Cooking

WILD GAME

AND FISH WITH

CHEF MILOS

Milos Cihelka

AuthorHouse™
1663 Liberty Drive
Bloomington, IN 47403
www.authorhouse.com
Phone: 1 (800) 839-8640

Published by AuthorHouse 10/12/2015

ISBN: 978-1-5049-4994-1 (sc)
978-1-5049-4996-5 (hc)
978-1-5049-4995-8 (e)

Library of Congress Control Number: 2015915479

Print information available on the last page.

authorHOUSE®

CONTENTS

PART 1   WILD GAME

PART 2   FISH AND SEAFOOD

INTRODUCTION

As an avid hunter, fisher or outdoorsman, you likely own top of the line equipment, take great pride in it, maintain it well and practice with it frequently. Whether bow, gun or rod, you are undoubtedly deadly accurate and head to a range, river, lake or maybe the deep sea frequently to hone your skills. But how much do you really know about the right way to transport, dress out, harvest, age and utilize all of the meat from your kills? How often do you get to practice the art of butchery? Probably not nearly as often as you get to practice your aim and accuracy.

About 15 years ago I attended an outdoor show in Novi, MI. One of the best attended seminars was hosted and produced by the Michigan DNR and was a full demonstration of how to properly slaughter and break down a freshly harvested white tail deer. The crowd was standing room only and nobody left during the entire 2 hour presentation, in fact people kept jamming in. As good as most hunters are at bagging their prey, they actually know very little and need help, instruction and practice in properly butchering and breaking down their latest trophy. There were lots of questions asked and many photos taken all through the process. Hunters hung around for quite a while afterwards asking all kinds of additional questions. It was apparent to me that most hunters don't really know what to do with a fresh kill, but really want to learn.

Realistically and unfortunately, very few outdoorsmen are skilled at this aspect of the hunt and harvest. Most don't really know that much about the anatomy of the animals that they hunt and even fewer know how to properly employ correct techniques to sanitarily field gut, transport and then hang, age, skin and break down an animal into a clean carcass. Much less do they know how to further break it down into primal and sub-primal cuts for total nose to tail complete utilization of the animal.

Assuming you want to learn these critical aspects of the hunt, then this book: "Cooking Wild Game and Fish with Chef Milos" is for you. Not only will you learn the proper, safe and sanitary way to break down your prize, but you will learn about complete utilization with excellent tips and unique methods to simplify the process. You will learn how to age, skin and bone out large and small game. You will also receive an extensive set of mouth watering, healthy and well tested recipes including stews, roasts, chops, and various charcuterie to add to your own repertoire and collection.

In "Fish and Seafood" segment you will learn simple techniques for handling fresh catches, purchasing tips, proper methods of holding and storing fish and seafood and lots of cooking techniques for freshwater and saltwater fin and flat fish, crustaceans, and shellfish.

And you will learn all of this from one of the best and most respected chefs, Certified Master Chef Milos Cihelka, who is himself an accomplished hunter and fisherman.

Chef Milos was born in Prague, Czechoslovakia, in 1930. He began his career as an apprentice pastry cook after graduating from High School at age 14. He next entered a second apprenticeship in cooking and by 19 held two journeyman diplomas in two different trades within the kitchen. Speaking fluent German and English, in 1950 he risked his life and escaped the grip of communism to West Germany where he continued cooking. In 1951 he immigrated to Canada cooking in fine hotels, private clubs and restaurants. He and his new wife Claudette came to the USA in 1958 briefly working in New Jersey and Connecticut before settling in Detroit. His first job in Detroit was Executive Chef at the Roostertail and then Detroit Athletic Club and The London Chop House.

Chef Milos joined Owner Reid Ashton as the Executive Chef & Partner of the famous Golden Mushroom Restaurant in Southfield, MI in 1976 a year after it opened. The Golden Mushroom earned many prestigious awards and was famous for many things during its reign as Michigan's finest restaurant until it closed in 2003. But perhaps it is best known and still recognized as the training ground for many culinarians, who received a start there in their very successful careers, some later becoming master chefs themselves.

Years ago, Chef Milos became the first American Culinary Federation Certified Executive Chef in the State of Michigan. In 1981 the ACF held the first ever test for a new even higher certification level, Certified Master Chef. Chef Milos was invited to participate in this class to test for CMC. Not only did he pass the 10 day long grueling test, he earned the crystal award as the chef with the overall highest score. Today there are only 68 CMC's in the nation and only 12% of those that have ever even attempted the test, actually pass.

During his career, Chef Milos entered numerous culinary competitions here and abroad. As a member of the 1972 US Culinary Team he won two Gold Medals in the Culinary Olympics in Frankfurt, Germany. Returning to the 1984 Olympics, he earned a Gold Medal with Distinction for a perfect score with eleven dishes in a single event. In 1986 Chef Milos became the first manager-coach of the Michigan Culinary Olympic Team. In a two year period of competitions in the US and abroad, the Team won a total of 44 Gold Medals, three Grand Prizes, and two Best of Shows, culminating with the Grand Prize in Gold in the 1988 Culinary Olympics.

Starting in 1995-96 and over the next six years Chef Milos and partner Jerry Chiappetta filmed a series of nine educational videos that were originally released in VHS format. These videos quickly became the most critically acclaimed specialty training videos on the subject of the complete processing care, aging, transporting, butchering and cooking of wild game, fish and seafood. Starting in 2006 and finishing in 2008 the tapes were condensed down to three DVD's: Wild Game Field Care & Cooking (225 minutes); Upland Small Game & Waterfowl Care and Cooking (226 minutes); and Fish & Seafood Care and Cooking (189 minutes). They are currently sold on Amazon.com and through www.wildharvestvideos.com.

Jerry Chiappetta, a well -respected sportsman and videographer served as the outdoor editor of The State Journal in Lansing and then became the Outdoor Editor at The Free Press. He appeared on WXYZ starting in 1968 with "Michigan Sportsman" and then acquired the "Michigan Outdoors" program around 1972 from Mort Neff, "The Great White Father," a pioneer of outdoorsman TV Shows. His film work has won 11 Teddy Roosevelt Awards from the Outdoor Writers of America.

These videos are still, to this day considered timeless and possibly the best training videos ever produced. I've personally owned these videos since they were first released and they contain some of the best training information I've seen since taking an Animal Science college level class. For years, Chef Milos was encouraged by many including myself to write text/training books that could be used in conjunction with these videos by avid outdoorsmen and culinarians alike to share these timeless skills and best practices.

After years of retirement and working to put this knowledge and skill to paper, this book now exists and will likely become some of the most important and well used reference material in any sportsman's library. It is designed to be used by both hunters and chefs. It is written to be understood at the basic level but includes the small details that you need to know to really utilize your products in the best possible ways with both simple and highly creative recipes sure to please anyone.

Brian F. Lorge, CCTP, HAAC
Executive Director
ACF Michigan Chefs de Cuisine
ACF Windy City Professional Culinarians
ACF Cleveland Chefs
Vice-Chairman, Secretary/Treasurer
World Food Travel Association

FOREWORD

Hunters and fishermen in the United States and Canada are fortunate to have such an abundance and variety of game and fish to pursue. The relatively low cost of permits and the ease of obtaining them, as compared to hunting in many other countries, is also remarkable. The ability to seek a variety of species in different states and provinces is difficult to compare.

What amazes me most is that for all of these advantages being available to us, only a small percentage of hunters and fishermen really know how to properly handle the game or fish they harvest. Most deer hunters don't want to handle their kill and take it to a processor. Many fishermen either release or give the fish away because they do not know how or do not want to clean it.

But the saddest thing to me is that so many people refuse to eat wild game, some even calling it "poor folk subsistence food". The only reason for this attitude is that these individuals have never eaten properly handled and cooked wild game. Because of bad experience, many hunters will have their deer made into salami and sausages. At our restaurant we featured a wild game dish on our dinner menu daily. Often, I have had a customer ask me: "Why is it, that when I bring home a deer, my wife refuses to cook it or have anything to do with it. And then we come to your restaurant and she orders the venison and loves it?!" I tried to explain, that long before the cooking starts, the deer has to be properly handled, aged and butchered. The cook cannot make miracles with badly handled game or fish.

My book is intended for use by chefs and those hunters and fishermen and their families and friends who desire to find a better way of enjoying their hard-earned harvest.

This book covers game aging. It seems that every time I mention this subject, some people in the audience make a face as though saying: "He is going to rot the meat!"

And yet these same people must have seen restaurants advertising they sell aged beef.

Indeed, even Wal-Mart now advertises "aged steaks"!

All animal species, a short time after they expire, stiffen with *rigor mortis*. Depending on their size and the ambient temperature, they will remain stiff for one to several days. Any animal processed during this time of stiffness will yield extremely tough meat. Even after relaxation, fresh meat will still remain tough. Worth mentioning is that the most tender meat will come from animals which have been shot from ambush and expire fast. Any animal, both wild and domestic, that has been chased before expiring, will have a large amount of adrenalin pumped into its muscles, making the meat tough. Deer harvested in agricultural areas, where good food is plentiful, will taste far better than those harvested in a cedar swamp.

After slaughtering, sections of domestic animals are hung in coolers for a week before fabricating. Afterward, most wholesale cuts are packed in heavy plastic bags, in which they *"wet age"*. In aging, enzymes present in all flesh will gradually break connective tissues tenderizing the meat and at the same time mellow the taste. Just as freshly made cheese or wine are not consumable, wild game is dramatically improved by aging.

Part One:

WILD GAME

SECTION: BIG GAME

SO YOU'VE HAD A SUCCESSFUL HUNT!

During medieval times in Europe, wild game was reserved for kings and noblemen. Peasants were not allowed to eat it and the penalty for poaching game was death! Even nowadays, wild game in Europe is still considered a delicacy, handled with great care and respect, reserved for special occasions and served in expensive restaurants. In the Unites States many people dislike eating wild game, having had bad experience with it.

The majority of hunters really do not want to have anything to do with the game after they harvest it, preferring to let someone else take over. Typically, the processor immediately skins the deer, then cuts off the head and feet and throws the carcass in the freezer. When frozen solid, it is then cut up on a band saw, with bones, fat and sinews in every cut. The result is strong, gamey tasting, tough meat unfit for cooking in any manner. No wonder it tastes bad!

If you are really determined to have great tasting, tender game, my book will guide you through the steps from A to Z. You do not need to be afraid of failure.

Most people who enjoy a tender, flavorful steak or delicious roast in a fine restaurant probably do not realize that the meat has been aged for three to six weeks. Wild game also needs to be aged, which you can accomplish easily yourself. But do not try to take aged deer to a processor, as they will refuse to handle it.

FIELD CARE OF BIG GAME

You should carry a drag rope in your pocket, or pack along with your knife a few plastic bags that zip close for transporting the organs, and some disposable arm-length plastic gloves. Big game should be field dressed immediately.

Quick field dressing facilitates cooling and prevents spoilage when the danger of the meat turning sour is especially high. This is critical during the warmer weather of early bow hunting season, or when hunting in a desert or hot, arid country for antelope, mule deer, black-tailed deer, wild boar or javelinas.

First, place a tag on the deer to make it legal according to your state regulations.

Begin gutting the animal. Start by inserting a knife with a 5 inch narrow blade at the edge of the rectum, just under the tail. The blade should enter straight in above the rectum, touching the spine. When the blade is fully inserted, with a sawing motion begin cutting around the perimeter of the rectum, touching the surrounding bones, severing the connective tissues that hold the colon. **Be careful not to cut into the intestine**. When finished, you should be able to pull out several inches of the colon.

Next, lay the deer on its back; it's helpful to ask someone to hold it in that position.

If not, you may tie a front leg to a tree or bush to hold it up. When it is a buck, remove the genitals. Locate the sternum (center end of the rib cage). Carefully insert the point of the knife edge up, just through the skin and underlying membrane, exposing the cavity, but not cutting into the stomach. If your knife has a gut hook, insert it there and draw it all the way down to between the legs. Otherwise, insert two fingers of your free hand palm up into the opening. Holding the point of the knife edge up between your fingers, carefully open the abdominal cavity all the way down, taking care not to cut into the viscera.

Now, if you are right-handed, lay the deer on its right side, preferably on a slight incline, legs downhill. Pull the stomach, liver and intestines out, detaching any tissues which hold it in. Check to see that the urine bladder was removed (found in a cavity between the hind legs next to the spine), being careful not to burst it! Remove kidneys and excess fat. Check under the tail - there should be just an empty hole, no intestinal remnants.

Then cut through the diaphragm (membrane separating the lungs from the viscera). Put your left hand through this opening to the front of the chest as far as you can reach and grasp the heart. Carefully move the knife in your right hand forward; sever the trachea, esophagus and arteries above the heart, and then pull the heart and lungs out. Move the deer away from the gut pile, then flip it on its belly to drain the blood from the cavity. You can lift the front of the deer up to facilitate drainage. Spread the legs to keep it in that position and leave it draining for a while.

If you have punctured the viscera, the cavity needs to be flushed with cold water. If none is available at the moment, wiping the cavity with moss, grass or ferns will help temporarily. Upon arrival home, you should make certain that the cavity is clean. It is a good idea to wipe it out with a vinegar-soaked towel, which kills bacteria and eliminates odor.

The liver, heart, kidneys and also the testicles are all very much edible. These parts, along with the tenderloins, can be cooked immediately, especially if you are in a hunting camp. My section on "Fast Foods" gives recipes for the preparation of these quick camp meals.

PROCESSING

I recommend processing your venison yourself, rather than taking your kill to a commercial processor. A processor will weigh the deer and mark the weight on the receipt. Then they skin it, cut the head and feet off and freeze the whole carcass immediately. When frozen, it is cut up on a band saw like a loaf of bread, with every slice having bone, fat, sinews and various parts of meat. I was told it takes them about 8 minutes to cut up a deer! When the customer comes back to pick it up, they will give him the amount of meat or product according to his deer size. It will be anybody's deer, no matter where it came from or how that other hunter shot, cleaned and handled it. They do not have the time to tag and handle your deer separately. Venison processed in rigor mortis with bones and fat is unsuitable for any type of cooking. And it will turn rancid in the freezer in a couple of months. I have had hunters offer me such venison. Since I did not have dogs at that time, I thanked them and after they left, threw it away.

Once you have aged and processed your own deer and tasted the difference, you will never again take it to a processor. And when you serve it to your guests, they will not believe it is venison! I can guarantee you that, absolutely!

TRANSPORTATION OF BIG GAME

To drag a deer, first cross the front feet behind the head. Then attach the drag rope around the neck, holding the feet in place. The dragging is much easier this way. Larger game such as elk, moose or caribou necessitates quartering the animal on the spot and packing the meat on horseback, on your own back, by snowmobile or all-terrain vehicle.

When hanging game in camp or when transporting it home, make sure it stays dry and that air can circulate around the animal. It is not a good idea to put a still warm animal in the back of a heated station wagon or SUV for a long drive. If it starts raining or the road is extremely dusty and the deer is secured on the roof rack, cover it with a plastic – but never wrap it in plastic when the body is still warm.

For long distance transportation, it is very important to have the meat well chilled but not frozen. Chilling can be speeded up by inserting ice frozen in gallon jars, or bags of ice, into the cavity of a hanging animal. Do not allow ice or melting water to make direct contact with the cavity, which must remain dry. Once the meat has been thoroughly chilled, it will remain cold for up to three days in reasonably cool temperatures. We have transported big game to Michigan from Eastern Canada and Western states, just cold, not frozen.

One good way to get great results in a distant hunt area is to ask a local butcher to age the saddle and hind quarters (of an elk or moose as example), hanging them in his walk-in cooler. After 3 weeks, he can bone the meat out, pack it in plastic-lined cardboard boxes and ship it by air freight to you. It will not spoil! But do NOT allow him to cut it into steaks or freeze the meat. They usually do a terrible job! For best results, cut the steaks and roasts yourself, then freeze them.

Contrary to popular opinion, meat will not spoil very fast. Even small game, such as rabbits, ducks or pheasants, when properly chilled, can be transported in coolers just as they are, whole, with feathers on, un-gutted. I have done so on several occasions.

AGING GAME

As chef-owner of a restaurant that featured wild game on the menu daily, I often had customers ask why our game tasted so much better than the game they prepared at home.

I explained that long before the cooking starts, proper care of the harvested animal is of utmost importance – beginning with careful field dressing and then aging. It seems that everyone knows about aging beef, wine and cheese, but few understand the importance of aging wild game.

Most of you must have seen advertisements of restaurants claiming that they serve "dry aged beef". What does that exactly mean? Restaurants specializing in exceptional quality of steaks, roasts and also lamb have what is in the industry called "aging boxes". These are walk-in refrigerators dedicated to aging meat only, which means no other food products can be stored there. They are temperature and humidity controlled and have an ultraviolet light which inhibits the growth of bacteria. The meat must be in large pieces with bones, such as whole hind legs, sirloin shells or prime ribs. It is either hung from hooks or placed on perforated shelves and rotated daily. Small cuts and boneless meat cannot be dry aged. During aging, which lasts 3-6 weeks, the meat will lose weight through desiccation and the open ends will develop mold, necessitating extra trimming. All of that adds substantial cost to serving dry aged beef and lamb. Other domestic animal products are also aged. These include various types of salami, sausages and dry cured hams. The best and most expensive dry cured ham is produced in Spain. Some of these hams are aged for up to three years!

Besides dry aging, there is also "wet aging". Beef cuts, such as tenderloins, strip loins and lamb cuts, are vacuum packaged in thick plastic bags called "Cryovac". Refrigerated, meat in these bags will keep for several weeks and will also age to a degree. But the flavor and tenderness will not equal dry aging. So what happens in aging?

During aging, enzymes that are naturally present in all flesh gradually break down connective tissues, tenderizing the meat. At the same time, just as in aging wine or cheese, the flavor of the meat mellows with age. This is especially noticeable in wild game, which when cooked in a fresh state is tough and has a strong "gamey" taste.

While few sport hunters have access to walk-in coolers, most do have an airy garage or barn to use for aging game during the fall and winter hunting seasons in cooler climates. Even if the outside daytime temperature rises to 55° F and nighttime drops below freezing, the garage or barn will modify these swings. Keep a window open or place a small fan nearby to circulate air. Ventilation is important. If the temperature in your storage space drops below 28° F, protect hanging venison from freezing by loosely draping a tarp over it and turning on a light bulb or a small heater underneath. **Make sure you do not allow the carcass to freeze!**

A number of hunters who are successful every year, especially those living in warm climates, have built their own aging coolers. These can be simply constructed from plywood, insulated and equipped with a small-size air conditioner placed in a cut-out window. The cooler can be as small as 6'x6' and 8' high with a sturdy ceiling with hooks for hanging game. Friends, relatives or club members can share the cooler space and expense. The cooler can be located in a barn, garage, or any shady, protected location.

Hang the deer head-down and place a bucket under it to collect drainage. The reason for hanging it this way is that we don't want blood and bodily fluids to drain and pool up in the hindquarters during aging. You should also prop the cavity open with a stick between the flanks in order to allow air to circulate inside the body. Remember to remove the tenderloins on the inside, next to the spine, so they do not dry out. They can be cooked fresh.

The best temperature for aging is 40° F. Warmer temperatures will speed up aging; cooler temperatures will slow it down; freezing temperatures will stop aging. So in warm weather, you can shorten the aging time.

HOT OIL FLY REPELLANT

Big game hunting during warm weather can present a problem due to flies and other insects getting on the flesh when your animal is hung for draining and aging. To prevent this, I recommend using my formula for "hot oil," which you can easily make at home.

Similar chemical fly repellants are sold commercially as "liquid netting."

To **make your own hot oil**, place two cups of vegetable oil in a small sauce pan on the stove. Add a small handful of dried crushed red chili peppers. Stir. Allow the oil to start sizzling, and then remove it from the stove. Set aside to cool. Pour it into a jar and seal it. Store this in a cool place. It is not necessary to strain out the pepper flakes; the oil will get hotter with age. It will keep for a year without refrigeration.

Before you apply the hot oil, make sure the cavity of the animal is dry. If not, wipe it out with paper towels. Spill some oil into the palm of your hand and lightly coat the entire cavity, plus any openings such as the mouth, nose, eyes and shot holes where flies might enter. Pour a little extra down into the throat.

Do not oil the hide. The animal's hide is the best protection against flies and other insects. This hot oil formula will not affect the taste of the meat.

As your meat ages, check the cavity daily. It should remain dry to the touch. If slime develops, wipe it off immediately with a vinegar-soaked towel. The cavity will dry again in a day or two. After about seven to 10 days, you will notice white specks of mold on the exposed surface of the cavity. This is a normal occurrence and is nothing to be concerned about so long as the cavity remains dry. In two weeks the mold may cover the entire cavity and there will be a strong, unpleasant odor. Again, this is normal, nothing to worry about.

Hang a fawn or a doe for two weeks, a mature deer for three weeks and an old buck for up to four weeks. Only then should the animal be skinned and butchered.

Note: you cannot age any game or domestic meat after it has been frozen.

Let us then briefly cover the key points of aging large game before we move on to skinning, quartering and butchering:

- the animal is hung head down, chest cavity opened with a stick

- best temperature for aging: 40° F.

- cover with a tarp and use a light bulb beneath the tarp if temp is below freezing

- keep inside cavity dry and ventilated

- wipe away any slime with vinegar-soaked towels

- age young fawn or calf moose, elk or caribou one week

- age adult doe or cow elk, moose or caribou two weeks

- age mature buck or bull three to four weeks

- inspect the deer every few days for wetness

- don't worry about odor, it will have no effect on the meat

SKINNING BIG GAME

Several years ago, Jerry Chiappetta, a well-known producer of outdoor television series and myself produced nine tapes demonstrating processing and preparation of wild game, fish and seafood. These very popular tapes have won a number of awards and were later converted into DVDs, which are still available from Amazon. They are called Wild Harvest Videos and were judged the best of their type by American Culinary Federation. The videos are used in culinary schools and guide any individual, including housewives in game and fish processing and cooking.

Tools needed for skinning and butchering are available from restaurant and butcher supply stores: skinning knife, boning knife, sharpener and bone saw. You will also need a strong rope, large cutting board, plastic sheets or large metal trays, vacuum packing machine and bags.

Contrary to what you may have heard, skinning a deer right after the kill will not improve its flavor. It will only dry the meat out and result in additional waste. Removing the musk glands from the insides of the hind legs is another myth, as is cutting a deer's throat to "bleed it." These actions will make no difference in the taste of the meat.

The tenderloins, located inside the cavity on either side of the spine, should be removed soon after the animal has been harvested to prevent them from drying out. Tenderloins are tasty and tender even when fresh, so you can cook them right away.

One of the easiest ways to **skin a deer while it is hanging** is to use a vehicle to pull the hide off. First, however, make sure your deer is hanging head-down from a sturdy tree limb or strong beam in your garage or barn.

If you wish to have the head of a trophy animal mounted, slit the hide starting between the antlers, in a straight line along the top of the neck and the top of the spine. Then cut around the torso behind the shoulders, slit the hide on the inside of the front legs and pull the cape off up to the head. Cut the neck off just below the head, leaving the head attached to the hide. Always cut the hide with the edge of the knife pointed up to prevent cutting hair.

To skin the whole deer:

Split the skin from the center of the chest opening straight down to the chin. Starting below the knees slit the hide on the insides of the front legs up, through the arm pits, exiting in the cavity.

Slit the hide of the hind legs starting from the abdominal cavity, on the inside of the legs, up past the ankles. Pulling with your hand and pushing fingers under the hide– with some help from your skinning knife – peel the skin off the hind legs until you can reach all the way around each leg. Remove the tail. Then cut the hide off at the ankles and pull it down to the midsection of the deer. Make sure the flanks are free of hide.

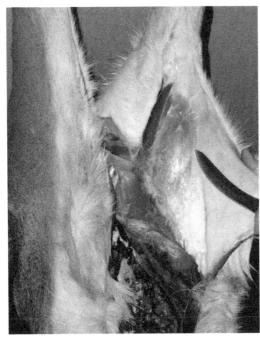

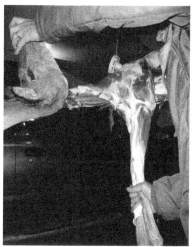
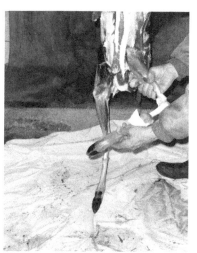

Attach a strong rope with a slipknot and a golf ball or 2 inch block of wood inside a gathering of the hide, then attach the other end of the rope to a vehicle. Have someone slowly back the vehicle away from the deer. Stand off to the side in case it breaks down. Alert the driver to stop the vehicle when the hide is pulled up to the head. While keeping rope tension on, use your knife to cut the skin off the front legs, below the knees, then cut through the neck muscles, the trachea and esophagus to the spine just below the head all around. Keep the rope tension on.

Holding the front legs with one hand to prevent spinning, grab the deer nose and forcibly twist the head around. The spine will snap off, and the head will drop down with the hide.

In this process, the deer hide will come off as easily as skinning a rabbit. Hides removed this way are excellent for making deerskin garments, as with care, there will not be a single knife cut on the hide.

BREAKING DOWN A BIG GAME ANIMAL IN 10 STEPS

1. Keep the animal hanging. Spread a sheet of plastic or place large trays within easy reach for offloading the venison parts as you remove them.

2. Lift a front leg and jab the point of a boning knife, edge up, into the inside of the knee. Sever the tendons, then cut the membrane all around the knee. Holding the upper part of the leg with one hand, grasp the part below the knee and twist sideways. The knee joint will pop out and remaining tissue can be cut off. Repeat on the other leg.

3. Use a knife to cut off the shoulders. Start cutting inside the armpit with one hand, while the free hand pulls the shoulder away from the chest. There is no bone connection (it's called "free floating"), but you will have to cut next to the rib cage up above the shoulder blade. Repeat.

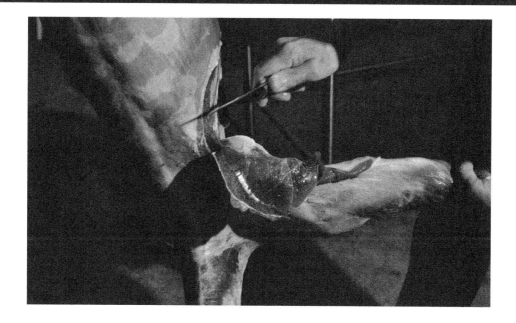

4. Use a saw to split the chest open down the center to the neck.

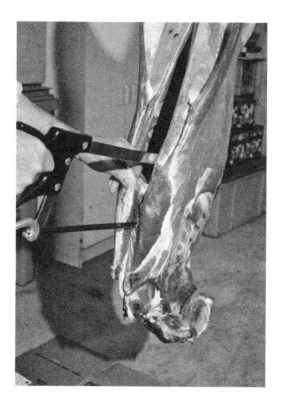

5. With a knife make a horizontal cut through the flank below the hind leg to within 4 inches of the spine. Then cut straight down, parallel to the spine, to the rib cage. Repeat on the other side.

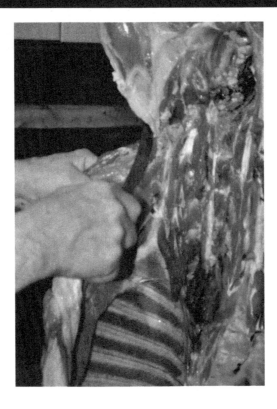

6. Use a saw to continue the cut straight across the ribs down to the neck to remove the rib cage. Repeat.

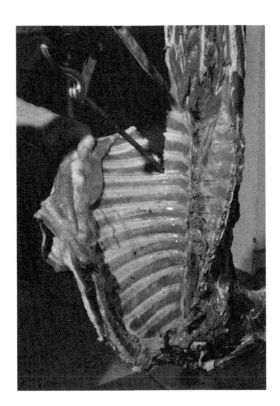

7. Use the saw to cut the neck off at the fourth vertebra up from the bottom of the chest.

8. Saw off the saddle (spine with back straps) at the third vertebra down from the hind legs.

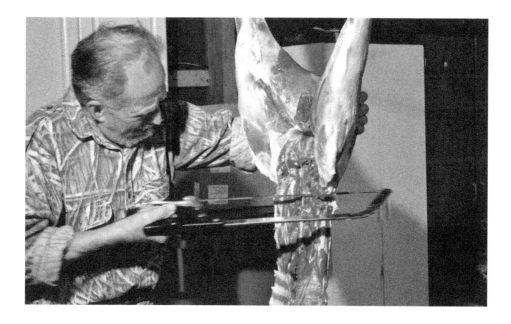

9. Saw the hind legs apart by cutting straight down between them.

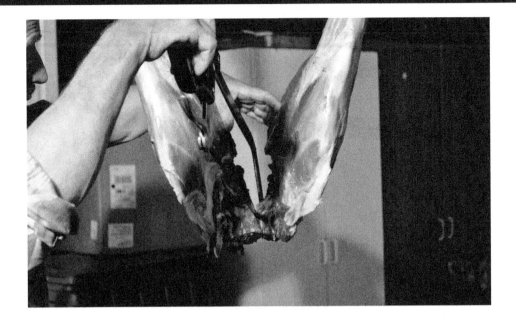

10. Saw off the hind feet at the ankles.

11. The parts are now ready for further butchering.

THE BUTCHERING PROCESS

All four-legged animals have the same basic bone structure. So once you debone a deer, you will notice the same kind and shape of bones in a rabbit or squirrel or bison. The size of the animal is the only difference between them.

THE HIND LEGS

Let's begin the deboning process, starting with the hind legs. There are basically three different types of muscles in the hind legs. Each is suited for different cooking preparations. Everyone knows that for a good steak or roast you need tender meat, but few people know that for the best stew and pot roast you need tough, sinewy meat!

Hind legs should be "seamed out" – which means separating the muscles one from another at the seams. Every muscle is wrapped in silver skin. The seams divide the muscles. To determine the tenderness of meat, pinch it hard with your thumb. If you are able to crush it by pushing the thumb into the meat, it is tender. If it feels like rubber, it is stew meat or pot roast.

To de-bone the hind legs, use a sharp boning knife. Place the leg with the inside up and the pelvis toward you. Follow these steps:

1. Hold the point of the knife toward the bone and make a shallow cut around the pelvic bone until you reach the ball joint from both sides, then free one end, lift the bone up and cut around the other end. Never cut too deep and **always keep the knife touching the bone.**

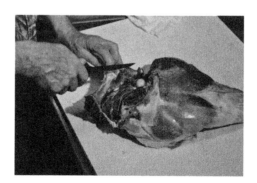

2. Turn the leg around and bone out the shank following the bone. Disconnect the bone off at the movable knee joint.

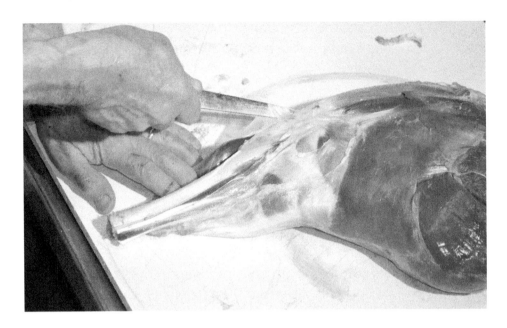

3. Locate the white line that runs down the center between the shank and the pelvis. Make a careful, shallow incision without cutting into the muscle.

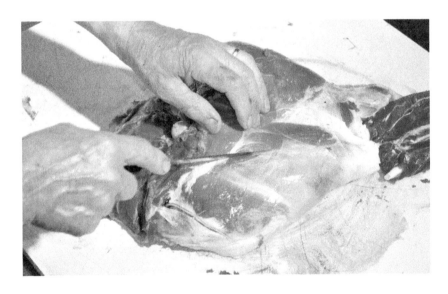

Follow the silver skin that covers the muscles. When you reach the bone, cut around it from both sides, then free one end, lift the femur bone up and cut around the other end.

The leg is now boneless except for the kneecap which is attached to the bottom butt.

4. **To separate the major muscles**, pinch with your thumb and fingers where they join together and disconnect them, pulling apart. Always follow the natural seams and don't cut into the meat itself.

5. After you have separated the muscles, sort them out according to their tenderness and cooking suitability:

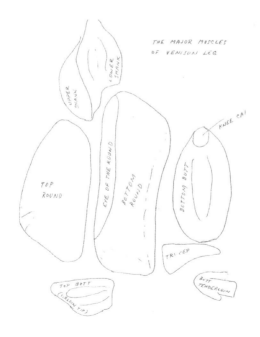

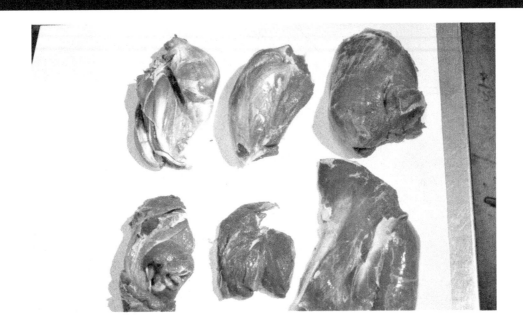

shanks: for stew, pot roast or grind

bottom round, eye of the round: roast or pot roast

top round, top butt and bottom butt: These are very tender muscles, suitable for steaks and roasts. They have "silver skins", some of which run deep into the muscle. These should be removed before roasting or grilling. Some tender muscles have "caps," which are smaller, thin pieces of attached meat. These caps are tough and for real enjoyment they should also be removed and used in stews or grind. To locate them, simply grasp the muscle and feel for the loose parts.

The meat of elk, moose, mule deer, blacktail deer, antelope or caribou is all called venison and should be handled in the same way as white-tailed deer, with the exception that the large animals are usually quartered before aging. A bear should be skinned before aging.

BONING THE SADDLE

The saddle section contains the best meat. On the inside are the tenderloins; on the outside, the loins, also called back straps. In beef, it would be the prime rib and sirloin strip.

To remove them, cut straight down along either side of the center bone, starting at the neck. When you reach the bottom, carefully flatten the knife to get it past the knuckles, then down again to the ribs. From there, just follow the rib bones out.

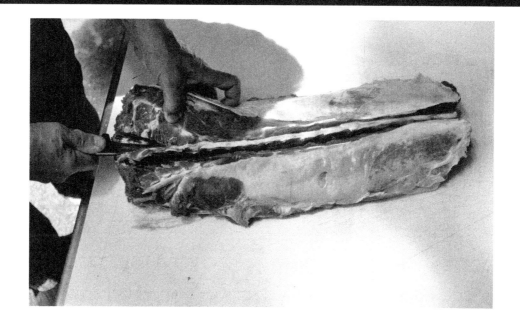

The loins have caps at the neck end that are tough and should be removed. They can be pulled off easily with a little help from a knife. The caps, when trimmed, can be used in stews or grind meat. The loins make great steaks or roasts. They also have small strings of meat attached on the spine side.

BONING OUT THE SHOULDERS

Using a boning knife, bone out the shank first. Next, turn the outside of the leg upwards and locate the ridge of the shoulder blade. Cut straight down along both sides. Level the knife and follow to the edge of the blade. Cut around and then under the bone, and remove it by disconnecting it at the joint. Finally, remove the center bone.

The two thickest muscles in the shoulder are the chuck. They make excellent pot roast. The rest of the shoulder is good for stew or grind.

BONING OUT THE NECK

To bone out the neck, start on the upper side and follow the "feather" bones of the vertebra down. As you reach the trachea and the esophagus, remove and discard them. The meat of the neck is layered with fat which should be removed. Neck is the toughest part of the deer and best used in stews or grind. You can also make a pot roast out of it by rolling it up and tying with a string. The bones make a good brown stock if combined with pork or chicken bones.

RIBS & FLANKS

If the deer has been aged, cut off the usable meat from the outside of the rib cage and discard the bones. There are several layers of meat and fat here to be removed before cooking. Once cleaned, the rib and flank meat is best used in stew or grind. It is the least desirable section of the deer.

Venison fat has a very bad taste, and should always be completely trimmed off and discarded before cooking. It has a high melting point and will congeal on your teeth and the roof of your mouth. It can be used raw in bird feeders.

FREEZING GAME

The marrow in bones is the first to turn rancid, permeating the meat with its nasty odor. For that reason, venison should always be boneless for home freezing. An exception would be whole legs. Vacuum machines that come with heavy plastic bags are the best freezer wrap solution. Any air left inside a package will result in freezer burn on your meat. Write the date and the cut of meat on the wrapping.

For best results, leave the meat in whole muscles, silver skin on, untrimmed. Close trimming or cutting into steaks will result in loss of moisture and greater freezer damage. The time to remove the silver skin and cut it into steaks is just before cooking, but do remove the fat, as it might turn rancid.

When freezing game, do not stack packages on top of each other. It is important that they freeze fast. Less freezer damage will occur. Once frozen hard, they may then be stacked. Properly butchered, deboned and sealed venison will keep well for more than a year.

For cooking pot roasts and stews, leave the heavy sinews and silver skin on for protection against drying out during the lengthy cooking process. They are made of a protein called collagen, which during slow, moist cooking softens to a gelatinous consistency, which makes the meat very pleasant to eat.

Stew meat is difficult to brown once it has been frozen, so I prefer to make a big batch of stew from the trimmings, neck, flanks and shanks the day after I have butchered the deer. I let the cooked stew cool off, then package it in desired servings in plastic cups or bags and freeze it. It keeps well and is very convenient later. My wife loves this idea!

HAMBURGER

Venison is very lean. When making hamburger, you will need to add either beef suet or fresh pork fat in the proportion of one pound of fat to five pounds of venison. Ground meat does not freeze well, so I recommend freezing chunks of meat and grinding and blending it before cooking.

Also, hamburger of any kind is best made from fresh meat, not aged or frozen.

FAST FOODS

An invitation to join a group of deer hunters on private property, stipulating that I would cook the first dinner for them, was too good to pass up. In the morning of the first day, I told all of them to save me the liver, heart, kidneys and testicles of any bucks they shot. Most complied with the livers and hearts, just a couple of them saved the rest.

In the evening, as I was getting ready to prepare the items, a fellow I was only introduced to as Steve, asked me if he could help me skin and devein the livers. I reluctantly agreed, not wanting to hurt his feelings, but was worried he would shred them. To my amazement, he did a great job! Curious, I asked him what he did for a living. He said he was a surgeon!

I cooked all of it in stages in a huge skillet with bacon fat, then piled it up on a platter. Everyone took the liver and heart, but it took some persuasion to get them to try the kidneys and testicles. After they realized how great they tasted everyone wanted more, but there was not enough to go around.

TENDERLOINS

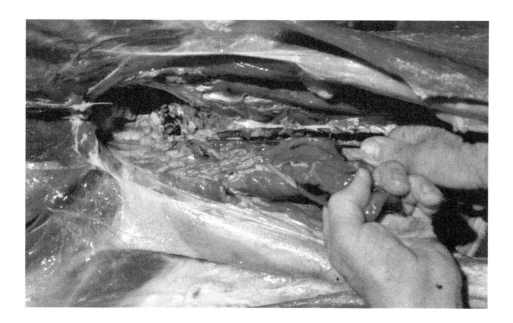

Tenderloins are the most tender cuts of meat on any animal. They should be removed from the carcass before you age it as otherwise they will dry up in a few days. Trim away all silver skin, cut the tenderloin into 3 inch long pieces, then stand these up and flatten them down to ¾".

Grill or pan fry fast to rare or medium rare. Overcooking will make the meat dry. Tenderloins are also tasty when stir-fried.

The "offal", or varietal meats as they are known, is the heart, liver, kidneys and testicles. They are best cooked within a couple of days after an animal is harvested.

HEART

To prepare the heart, first rinse it thoroughly and trim away all surface fat. Split the chambers open, then cut away the sinews. Press the heart flat and cut horizontally into 1/3 inch thick slices.

Season the slices of heart with salt and pepper and coat with a little vegetable oil. Grill or pan-fry over high heat to medium rare, not well done, or the meat will be tough as shoe leather. Tastes like a steak!

LIVER

Rinse the liver and skin it. No need to look for a gall bladder; deer do not have one. Remove all large veins. Cut the liver into 1/3 inch thick slices. Again, season it with salt and pepper, moisten with vegetable oil and grill to medium rare. You may also sauté it in bacon fat. Overcooking will make both liver and heart tough and dry.

To sauté, dip the seasoned liver in flour and pan-fry quickly in bacon fat until browned on both sides. Serve with sautéed onions, peppers and mushrooms.

KIDNEYS

Split them horizontally then peel the outer membrane off. Place them cut side down, grab the protruding tubes and slice these off. Season the kidneys with salt and pepper and either grill or sauté to medium rare only. Serve with hot mustard. Mmm, I love them!

TESTICLES (ALSO CALLED "MOUNTAIN OYSTERS")

Remove them from the hairy pouch, then slit and peel the tough outer skin. Next, cut them horizontally into halves. Season, dust with flour and sauté in a medium hot skillet to done. They taste like veal sweetbreads! Excellent!!!

STIR-FRY OF TENDERLOINS

4 servings

This is a quick, simple dish to prepare in hunting camp using fresh tenderloins.

4 cups trimmed, tender venison, cut into ½ inch thick slices

3 Tbsp vegetable oil - peanut oil is best

2 cups sliced mushrooms

2 Tbsp finely chopped garlic

1 Tbsp grated fresh ginger

2 cups sliced onions

2 cups sliced red and green peppers

4Tbsp soy sauce

1 Tbsp corn starch dissolved in 3 Tbsp dry sherry wine

Have all ingredients at hand. Preheat a large skillet or wok until smoking hot. Add oil and quickly spread meat over the bottom in one layer without crowding. You may have to do this in two or more batches, making sure you clean and reheat the pan every time before adding meat. Do NOT stir the meat.

Sear the meat brown over high heat on one side, turn over and sear the other side for a few seconds. This should not take more than 15-20 seconds in total; the meat must remain rare.

Remove meat from pan. Add more oil if necessary and put the vegetables, mushrooms and garlic in. Sauté until heated through and vibrant in color. Do NOT cook! Season with pepper, soy sauce and cornstarch-wine slurry. Return meat to skillet, stir and serve immediately accompanied by rice, noodles or bread.

Note: you may not need to add salt, as the soy sauce is salty.

BROWN STOCK

Great-tasting sauces do not happen by accident. Serious cooks know that the difference between a great sauce or soup and a mediocre one is in the stock used to make it. For rich, delicious brown gravies, brown stock does wonders.

Brown stock is time-consuming, but the results are worth the effort. You can consider making a large batch of brown stock on a rainy day off. It is not very difficult to make. If you have a lot of oven space, make a double batch! Try to buy pork or veal neck bones for this stock, as they have some meat on them. Add any game bones you have. Chop all into small pieces.

Add an equal amount of chicken necks and backs to game bones for a better-tasting game stock.

You can speed up the brown stock by using only chicken backs and necks; you only need to simmer these for 2 hours to obtain a delicious chicken-flavored brown stock.

10 lbs bones: veal, pork, chicken or game combined	2 large onions, coarsely cut
1 lb pork skins, fresh or smoked. Water to barely cover	2 carrots, coarsely cut
3 cloves garlic	2 branches of celery, coarsely cut
30 black peppercorns	1/2 cup tomato puree
3 bay leaves	a pinch of thyme

Chop bones into small pieces and place them in a large roasting pan, along with the skins. Add about an inch of water. Place in an oven heated to 450° F to roast.

As the bones brown on top, turn them over so that they all brown evenly. When the water has evaporated and a brown glaze forms on the bottom of the pan, add another inch of water and continue the roasting and turning.

Repeat this process one more time, adding water as it evaporates. When the last of the water evaporates and the bottom of the pan is browned, transfer the bones into a large pot. Drain the fat from the pan and set aside.

On your stovetop, add water to the pan. Bring it to boil and deglaze all drippings, scraping the pan clean. Add the drippings to the pot. Fill the pot with enough cold water to barely cover the bones and bring it to a simmer. Skim the scum off.

Simmer slowly, skimming occasionally, for three hours. Brown vegetables in the fat drained from the bones, add to the stock, and cook for 30 minutes. Add puree and seasoning, and then cook for another 30 minutes. Strain through a fine strainer or cloth. Set to cool overnight.

This is now a brown stock. In order to be able to store it in convenient amounts, it is best to reduce it down to a concentrate. To do so, skim the fat from the surface and discard. Cook your stock down, boiling rapidly, until less than a quarter of the volume remains. Pour it into a shallow pan, cool. When cold, you can cut this jellied concentrate into small cubes. Wrap them individually in plastic, store in a plastic cup and freeze for future use.

This product is called "glace de viande" in French, or meat glaze in English. A cube or two added to a brown sauce will reward you with rich taste.

Note: venison bones alone do not make a great brown stock. I recommend that a blend of pork, veal, or chicken bones be added to venison bones, comprising at least half of the stock ingredients.

THE MOOSE HUNT

A friend of mine recommended a moose guide in Ontario with whom I booked a hunt. He was a very capable guide, but also a violator. The first thing he asked me was if I had a light on my bow! For the last day of my hunt, we flew to a remote lake in his cloth fuselage, two-seater Piper Cub. He tied the plane to shore, then we took a canoe to a tiny island where we spent the night, freezing in a pup tent. Every couple of hours, he stuck his head out and bellowed on his moose call. No response. In the early morning, in pitch darkness, we got as quietly as possible into his canoe and paddled slowly down the lake. When we reached a beaver dam, we heard crashing as a moose took off. Daylight was creeping in and the guide quietly dropped me off on the shore, while he went in his canoe around a bend. There he started wailing like a lovelorn cow moose. About twenty minutes later, I heard breaking branches. Hiding inside the brush, I could see the bull's antlers swaying side to side as he was making his way down to the lake, grunting with every step. He stopped at the edge of the lake to take a drink about 28 yards away. As I stood up, he looked at me surprised and I took the shot. The arrow passed through his chest, he made a great leap into the lake and started swimming across. Probably realizing he was not going to make it, he soon turned and tried to swim back, then expired. Only his antlers were visible above the water line. I was told that a lung shot moose lose the air and could sink, so I yelled at my guide to come over fast. He tied a rope to the moose's antlers and attempted to paddle to shore. Have you ever tried to paddle a canoe with a moose tied to the stern? Fortunately, he was not too far out, so with no alternative, I had to help him.

I waded into the freezing water up to my chest. Reaching for his outstretched paddle, I pulled him and the canoe. We then managed to pull the moose closer to shore, but we hit a sunken log and could not move him anymore. Fortunately, the guide had a small chain saw in his plane and after I gutted the moose out, the guide cut it into quarters in the water. The weight of each piece was incredible. Good thing the guide was built like a weight lifter.

On the shore he cut a small spruce to make a cross beam between two trees, lifted each quarter and I tied them up with the rope. Then he announced he was a little low on gas for his plane, but had some friends in a distant camp from whom he could "borrow" some. He instructed me to start skinning the moose, promised to be back soon and left.

I did the skinning job, ate some snacks and waited for his return. Eventually, as it started to get dark, I was preparing to spend the night by the moose to protect it from bears. I was thinking my pilot must have crashed somewhere. Suddenly, I heard a faint buzz, almost like a mosquito and he was coming in. What a relief!

The plane could not carry the whole moose. I sat behind the pilot with my seat removed, on top of a moose quarter, bent over, my head jammed against my bow attached to the ceiling above me and shoulders touching the fuselage. The moose rack was tied to the floats.

My pilot admitted his license to fly passengers was revoked. It appeared half of his instruments, except the gas gauge, did not even work, so he flew low following a river, barely visible in the faint star light. We landed on some small lake, beached the plane and he called his wife to come and pick us up. It was a hunt to remember!

CLASSIC VENISON ROAST

with sour cream sauce

For a roast that is to be served at medium rare, select either the loins or the tender muscles of the hind legs. Trim off all sinews and silver skin. Using Marinade 1, marinate the boneless meat for two to three days. Whole saddles or legs will need to marinate for one week.

Prepare the sauce in advance, using:

Drained vegetables from the marinade (about 1 cup)	1 cup sour cream
3 Tbsp bacon fat	1 cup brown stock or rich beef broth
1/2 cup marinade liquid	1 Tbsp mustard
2 tsp light soy sauce	3 strips lemon peel
1 Tbsp flour	

In a heavy-bottomed non-aluminum saucepan, sauté the vegetables in the bacon fat until they begin to brown. Add the liquid and simmer uncovered for 20 minutes. Mix the flour into the sour cream and whip it into the boiling juices. Add the rest of the ingredients and simmer 10-15 minutes more. Strain through a fine strainer or blend in a blender and then strain. Taste and correct seasoning. Keep warm.

For the roast:

Preheat the oven to 350° F.

Preheat a heavy skillet or roasting pan. Wipe the meat dry, and season with salt and pepper. Pour a little vegetable oil or bacon fat in the hot skillet and place the meat in.

Brown it quickly on all sides, and then move the pan and its contents into the oven. Roast for about 12 minutes per pound, or to an internal temperature of 115° -120° F*. Remove the roast from the oven and allow it to rest for 15 minutes before carving. Always slice across the grain.

Deglaze the pan drippings by adding the sour cream sauce to them and simmering gently.

*When you intend to serve any kind of beef, lamb or game roast Medium Rare, you need to remove it from the heat source when the internal temperature reaches not more than 120 F.

As the roast rests, (the bigger the cut, the longer it has to rest) the outside temperature radiates inwards. This is called *carry-over cooking,* and the meat will attain it's typical rosy color.

To serve:

Spill some of the sauce on a plate, placing sliced meat over it. Serve with spaetzles, noodles, or dumplings and braised red cabbage.

Note: you can make a delicious pot roast with this same sauce, using the thick part of the front leg (the chuck). Marinade as above, and proceed similarly as in my pot roast recipe (below), substituting the above ingredients.

VENISON POT ROAST

with red wine and currant jelly

3 lbs boneless shoulder

1 cup dry red wine

1 sliced carrot

1 sliced root parsley

1 sliced celery rib

1 medium onion, sliced

3 bay leaves

1 pinch thyme

1 pinch rosemary

1/4 cup clarified butter

salt to taste

1 cup rich beef broth

1/2 cup red currant jelly

2 Tbsp lemon juice

3 Tbsp brandy

1/2 cup heavy cream

3 Tbsp corn starch

2/3 cup port wine

2 Tbsp cracked black peppercorns

6 allspice berries

Marinate the meat with the wine, vegetables and spices in a glass, plastic, ceramic or stainless dish for a day or two. Keep tightly covered and turn the meat daily.

To cook: preheat oven to 325° F. Remove meat from marinade and wipe dry. Preheat a large skillet, add butter and brown the meat on all sides. Season with salt and transfer to a wide saucepan with a cover.

Drain the vegetables from the marinade and add them to the same skillet in which you browned the meat.

Brown the vegetables and then add the liquid from the marinade and the beef broth to the vegetable mixture. Bring all to a boil, pour over the meat, cover and place in the oven.

Cook for approx. 2 1/2 to 3 hours, depending on the age of your deer, turning the meat periodically until it gets fork-tender. Transfer to another dish, cover and keep warm.

Strain the cooking juices into a smaller saucepan, discarding vegetables. In a separate dish, dissolve corn starch in port wine. Add the result to the juice and bring to a boil. Add the rest of the ingredients, and taste to correct seasoning.

Serve with spaetzles, noodles, dumplings or polenta.

Note: do not use aluminum utensils when cooking with acids.

VENISON STEW

6 servings

Marinade:

1 large onion, sliced	2 Tbsp chopped garlic
1 Tbsp dried thyme	3 Tbsp crushed black peppercorns
6 crushed juniper berries	2 bay leaves
1/2 bottle dry red wine	3 1/2 lbs venison neck, or shanks cut into 2 inch cubes

Place all ingredients except the meat into a deep plastic, glass or ceramic dish and mix well. Add the meat and mix again. Cover tightly and refrigerate for one to two days.

1/2 cup clarified butter	salt
1 lb lean type slab bacon cut into 1inch cubes	4 Tbsp of tomato paste
1 cup rich brown stock	1 cup or more ginger snaps, crushed (for thickening)

Drain the wine off from the meat and reserve. Remove the onions from the meat and pat the meat dry, reserving the onions.

Preheat two large skillets. Put a dab of butter in each and divide the bacon between them. Cook the bacon until lightly browned and using a slotted spoon transfer it to a heavy non-aluminum saucepan, leaving the grease in the skillets.

Return skillets to the fire, heat up, add meat in single layers and over high heat brown it well on all sides. Do not stir the meat but allow it to brown on one side, then turn it over. With a slotted spoon, transfer the browned meat to the saucepan that contains the bacon. Place drained onions in the heated skillets and brown lightly. Add stock, salt, tomato paste and wine from marinade. Bring this mixture to a boil and pour over the meat. Bring it to a simmer, cover and simmer very slowly until tender. Depending on the age of the animal and type of meat, this could take between two and three hours.

When the meat is done, transfer it into another pot, leaving the onions and spices behind in the juice. Add ginger snaps, cook for five minutes and then strain, pressing hard over the meat.

Garnishes such as vegetables or mushrooms can be added to the stew. It is best to cook them slowly in a little butter separately, before adding them to the finished stew. Serve with noodles, spaetzles, boiled potatoes or crusty bread.

Note: aluminum pans are not suitable for cooking food with any acid content such as wine, tomatoes, etc. The flavor will be noticeably altered, and corroded aluminum is poisonous.

VENISON SKILLET STEAKS

Steaks can be cut from the loins, muscles of hind legs, or tenderloins. Cut as thick as desired. Season with salt and pepper.

Preheat a large skillet containing clarified butter or oil. Add steaks and sauté over high heat to desired state of doneness. Do not overcook.

Transfer steaks to a platter. Pour off the excess fat from the pan, add chopped garlic and green onions or chives, and stir.

Add a little dry red wine to dissolve the drippings, then add butter and stir briskly over high heat. Pour the resultant sauce over your steaks.

VENISON STEAKS WITH MUSHROOMS

4 servings

4 to 8 venison steaks

salt and pepper

3 Tbsp clarified butter

1/2 lb fresh mushrooms, sliced

1 Tbsp chopped shallot or 2 Tbsp chopped scallion

1/3 cup Madeira or dry sherry wine

1/3 cup heavy cream

Preheat either one large skillet or two medium-sized ones. Season steaks with salt and pepper. Pour butter into skillet and add steaks immediately. Brown on one side and turn over. Cook as desired. Transfer to a platter and keep warm. Place shallots and mushrooms in the still-hot skillet and sauté, stirring until mushrooms turn grey.

Add wine and continue cooking over high heat until most juice is evaporated. Add cream and cook down until it becomes a sauce. Pour over steaks.

Serve with sautéed potatoes, simple green vegetables or a salad such as a Caesar, or serve with Byron potatoes and roasted tomatoes.

GRILLED VENISON STEAKS WITH GRILLED POTATOES

When the outside temperature is agreeable, this item is our usual Sunday dinner with family. If you age your deer, then the tender muscles of the hind legs will be very tender and juicy. Trim off all silver skin, cut the steaks fairly thick, then flatten them slightly with a meat mallet. Mash some garlic, about one large clove to every two steaks. Crush or grind some black pepper. Put both into a non-reactive pan and add about one tablespoon of each per steak, a good soy sauce (we use Kikkoman) and vegetable oil. Stir this into a slurry, then coat the steaks with it. Cover the pan with plastic and refrigerate for several hours before grilling.

Light the grill. Wash some large potatoes, but do not peel them. Slice them length-wise into ¼ inch thin slices. Drizzle a small amount of oil on them, rub the slices together to spread the oil, but do not season them (salt would turn them wet).

Let the grill get fairly hot (I use charcoal). Leave one side a little cooler. Line up the potatoes on the hot grill, side by side. Allow them to brown on one side, flip over and brown on the other side. Then stack them on the cooler edge of the grill, where they will continue cooking.

Place the steaks on the grill and cook to desired doneness, rare to med. rare.

Note 1: the soy sauce is quite salty, so I do not add salt to the steaks. You may want to season the cooked potatoes though.

Note 2: using olive oil for grilling is wasteful, as the high temperature destroys it's delicate flavor. Any good vegetable oil is suitable.

ELK STEAKS WITH PEPPER & ROQUEFORT

6 servings

6 steaks cut from the back straps, about 2 inches thick

3 Tbsp crushed black peppercorns

salt

2 Tbsp olive oil or clarified butter

3 Tbsp chopped shallots

1 Tbsp chopped garlic

2 Tbsp cognac

1/2 cup brown stock

1/2 cup Roquefort cheese, crumbled

Flatten the steaks to about 1 inch thick. Place the whole pepper on a cutting board and crush using a heavy skillet or saucepan and a sliding motion with pressure, or use a spice grinder.

Season the steaks with salt and coat with pepper, pressing it into the meat.

Preheat a large skillet, pour the fat in, and add steaks. Over medium heat, brown them well on one side, then turn over on the other side and finish to desired doneness, preferably medium rare. Remove to plates or a platter.

Add shallots and garlic to the pan. Swirl them around, but do not allow them to brown. Add cognac and brown stock. Bring to boil, reduce a little, and then remove from fire. Whip in the Roquefort, and pour the final mixture over your steaks. Serve with sautéed potatoes, roasted vegetables or an Indian salad

VENISON CHILI CON CARNE

6 servings

1 cup dry red kidney beans

Pick the beans over, wash and either soak overnight in cold water or bring to a boil and cook for 10 minutes and remove from heat. Let stand for one hour, and then return to stove. Cook beans in unsalted stock or water until tender. Set aside.

Or: use 3 cups canned beans.

2 Tbsp corn oil	2 tsp coriander, ground
3 strips bacon, cut into 1/4 inch pieces	1/4 tsp cayenne pepper (or more if you like it hot!)
1 1/2 lb venison cut into ½ inch cubes	2 Tbsp cumin powder
2 cups chopped onions	1 1/2 Tbsp red wine vinegar
2-3 mashed garlic cloves	3 cups canned crushed tomatoes
1 large green pepper, chopped	3/4 cup brown stock (or water mixed with 2 bouillon cubes)
6 Tbsp chili powder	salt to taste

In a heavy saucepan, cook the bacon in oil until it starts to brown. Add the venison and cook, stirring until meat turns grey. Add onions, garlic and peppers and cook to translucent. Add spices and cook for one minute, stirring. Add the rest of the ingredients. Cook until meat is tender. If you want a thicker consistency, mix 3 Tbsp corn starch with a little water and stir into cooking chili. Stir in the red beans.

VENISON STROGANOFF

6 servings

1/2 cup clarified butter	3 cups sour cream, room temperature
2 lbs trimmed tenderloin or top butt cut into strips or slices 1/3 inch thick	4 Tbsp hot mustard
1 qt sliced fresh mushrooms	salt and pepper
2 cups onions, halved and cut into ¼ inch strips	

Preheat a large skillet or two to very hot. Add a little butter and put in no more meat than will cover the bottom of the pan. Do not stir! Over high heat, sear the meat on one side to brown. Turn over and sear it about 15-20 seconds on the other side. Remove meat from the pan **while rare**. (If you do this in batches, the pan must be clean and very hot before you add more meat. If you overload the pan the meat will start boiling in its own juice and will not brown.)

After all the meat is browned, add the mushrooms and onions to the same skillet and, if necessary, add more butter. Cook until mushrooms and onions become limp. Drain and reserve the juice.

Add the mushrooms and onions to the meat. Return the juice to the pan and whisk in the sour cream and mustard. Bring to a simmer. Season the meat with salt and pepper, then fold it into the simmering sauce. Stir and serve it immediately over noodles or spaetzles.

SMOKING VENISON

There are two basic smoking techniques – hot and cold. Hot smoked foods are cooked in the smoker. These include various sausages, also fish. Cold smoked foods are not cooked in the smoker. Examples of cold smoked foods are ham and salmon (lox). Some of these may be cooked after smoking (regular ham, picnics), some will remain only cured and cold smoked (salmon), some will be cured, cold smoked and dried (country and Westphalian hams). All smoked items must be cured with salt first to prevent bacterial growth.

COLD SMOKED VENISON

Note: Hot smoking will result in a dry venison, not very pleasant to eat. For this reason I prefer to cold smoke the venison, then roast it to med. rare afterwards. Smoke only tender cuts.

In cold smoking, the smoker temperature must not exceed 85° F. Commercial smokers are temperature controlled (refrigerated). To accomplish cold smoking at home, the weather must be fairly cold. The smoke generator can be placed some distance from the smoker to dissipate heat. The smoke can also be piped in through an ice bath to cool it down. A pan with ice may also be placed in the smoker and periodically replenished.

Note: **Cure** (also called "pink salt") is a combination of nitrites and salt. It is a basic preservative used to cure all meats, which require salting, smoking or canning. The basic formula for use with sausage: per 10 lbs of meat and fat, use two level teaspoons of pink salt mixed with six tablespoons of kosher salt. Cure, fermento, sausage casings and dextrose are available in hunting equipment or butcher supply stores along with a brining pump, bone saw, boning knives, etc., which you will also need.

For smoking, use venison that has not been frozen. The best-suited parts are the hind legs, separated into individual muscles. The silver skin covering the muscles should be left on to protect the meat from drying out. Weigh each individual piece of the meat and write the weight down._You will need this information when brining the meat.

The recipe below is **per each pound** of meat. Multiply the **total weight** of meat you intend to smoke by the fractions listed below. You can dissolve the honey in a small amount of hot water and then make up the remaining with ice-cold water, as long as the finished temperature of the brine is 38-40° F when curing begins.

Brine: (per pound of meat)

0.88 cup water

0.08 oz cure (nitrite)

2.00 oz honey

0.64 oz salt (pickling or kosher)

0.24 oz dextrose

Stir together to dissolve.

Fill the pump with the brine, insert the needle into the meat and inject the brine in. Hold the meat over the container with the brine. Insert the needle at 2 inch intervals, injecting brine until the meat can't hold any more.

Place the meat in a stainless, glass or plastic container. When done pumping, pour the remaining brine over the meat and keep at 40° F. **Brine each individual piece for three hours per pound**, and then remove, rinse and place on a refrigerator rack to dry. Once dry, rub a little cooking oil all over it and cold smoke (at less than 85° F.). The smoking time will depend on the density of smoke and the intensity of flavor desired, usually several hours. You will experiment.

After smoking, sear the meat on all sides in a hot skillet or roasting pan and roast at 350° F. to an internal temperature of 115° F., or medium rare. This will result in moist smoked venison, which can be thinly sliced. Hot smoking or overcooking will produce a dry, crumbly product.

Smoked venison can be served warm or cold. It is usually accompanied with a somewhat sweet sauce, such as a ginger sauce, or a refreshing relish, such as my apple horseradish relish.

VENISON JERKY

Jerky can be prepared from the meat of any member of the deer family, as well as from beef. I do not recommend making jerky from bear or wild boar meat, unless it has been treated to destroy trichinae and other parasites.

Jerky can be dried using various methods: a smoker, a fruit dehydrator, an oven, an attic, or, in dry climates, with only sun and wind. Smoking jerky is not necessary, but a light smoke will add to its flavor.

Preparation:

It is not necessary to use good cuts for jerky, but the meat should be trimmed of all fat, sinews and gristle. The best method, one in which you can utilize even small scraps of meat, is to prepare your meat by grinding it. All commercially produced jerky is fabricated in this manner. That is why all the slices are of uniform size.

Grind the venison on a ¼ inch grinder plate, and then mix thoroughly with the following ingredients:

For each 3 lbs of venison, mix together:

1 Tbsp salt (pickling or kosher is best)	1 Tbsp dextrose or granulated sugar
1/4 tsp curing salts (nitrate)	1 tsp garlic powder
1 tsp ground black pepper	

If you want a very spicy jerky, add 1 tsp of cayenne pepper.

Sprinkle this mixture over the meat and mix.

Add:

½ cup soy sauce

2 Tbsp Worcestershire sauce

Mix to blend well again. Cover and refrigerate for 24 hours.

Line a rectangular loaf pan with a **wet** plastic wrap, leaving overlap. Pack the meat in, pressing down to eliminate air pockets. Cover and place it in your freezer overnight. Then unmold the slab and, using a waverly-edged sharp bread knife, slice it through the wrap into ¼ inch thick slices.

Drying:

Coat wire racks or screen with oil or other non-stick spray. Remove the plastic and spread the slices flat, taking care not to overlap them. If you use a smoker or an oven, keep the temperature below 100° F. Keep the oven door slightly open to allow vapor to escape. The jerky will dry in three to four days. Jerky should never be dried to the point that it crumbles, but only to a leathery consistency.

Storing:

The jerky can be stored in a jar or a plastic container covered only with cloth. Always leave some openings - tightly closed containers will encourage the growth of mold. For jerky, refrigeration is not necessary, but for longer periods of storage you can freeze your jerky in a tight wrapping.

VENISON POLISH SAUSAGE

10 lb batch

IMPORTANT: When making forcemeats (sausage mixes), always maintain the meat temperature below 40° F. You may even partially freeze the meat before grinding it and chill the grinder parts before using them. During grinding and mixing, heat develops due to friction. Maintaining good sanitation during processing assures a safe product. It is best to use fresh meat. Do not use previously frozen meat.

6 lbs lean venison	2 Tbsp dextrose
4 lbs pork butt (with fat)	2-3 cloves of garlic, mashed
1 1/2 qts water	2 tsp curing salt
2 cups soy protein concentrate	1 Tbsp ground black pepper
6 Tbsp salt (pickling or kosher)	2 tsp marjoram

Trim heavy sinews and fat from the venison, removing any blood clots. Grind all meat on a 3/16 inch grinder plate.

Add seasonings to water and mix until smooth. Let your meat sit (refrigerated) in the mixture for a while to allow it to absorb the water. Stuff into hog casings.

Curing and Smoking:

Spread the sausage and leave at room temperature for one hour to dry. Hang in a smoker preheated to 120° F. for an additional hour, leaving a little opening for ventilation. Then increase the heat to 160° F. and smoke the meat to an internal temperature of 152° F. Remove and cool.

Keep smoked products refrigerated, wrapped in wax paper or parchment paper - but never in plastic - to prevent the growth of mold. Freeze for longer storage. Sausage can be eaten cold or heated.

To heat it in water, do not cut it. Leave the sausage whole until it is ready to be served.

The water temperature should not exceed 180° F., to prevent bursting of the casing. Yes, it will take longer to get it hot.

To grill, I recommend cutting the sausage into 3-4 inch segments, then cutting both ends about ½ inch deep (make 3 cuts crossing in the center in a star fashion on each end). By slow grilling, the ends will open up and the edges will get crispy. Serve with hot mustard.

VENISON SALAMI

10 lb batch

4 lb pork butt (with fat)

6 lb lean venison

2 cups ice water

2 cups soy protein concentrate

6 Tbsp salt (pickling or kosher)

1 tsp curing salt (nitrate)

1 Tbsp ground black pepper

2 Tbsp ground ginger

2 cloves garlic

6 Tbsp honey

Trim your meat of any heavy sinews or blood clots and partially freeze it. Have the grinder and all utensils pre-chilled as well. Grind the meat on a 3/16 inch plate.

Mix water with the rest of the ingredients, add to meat and mix well. Cover and refrigerate for 24 hours.

Remove from cooler and mix well.

Stuffing:

Stuff the venison salami tightly into either beef middles or a fibrous casing (which should be soaked in warm water for 20 minutes), trying to eliminate any air pockets. Puncture all air pockets visible under the casing with a needle and expel air. Hang the salami on smoker sticks and space apart in the smokehouse.

Smoking:

Open the smokehouse drafts wide. Preheat the smoker to 130° F. Hang the salami in without crowding and smoke, leaving a little ventilation for about 30 minutes, or till the surface of the salami is dry. Then raise the temperature in the smoker to 150° F. and an hour later increase it to 165° F. Continue smoking till the internal temperature of the salami reaches a minimum of 145° F. and a maximum of 152° F. Do not wrap until completely cold. Do not overcook the salami, or it will become dry and crumbly.

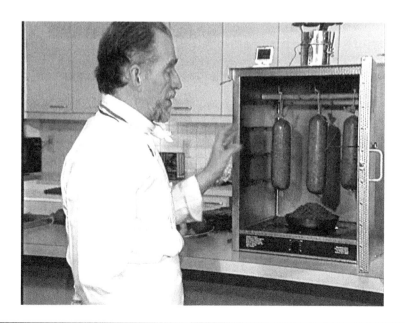

DRIED VENISON STICKS

10 lbs trimmed venison

4 Tbsp paprika

2 tsp cure

1 Tbsp mace

6 Tbsp dry mustard

1 tsp granulated garlic

1 tsp ground black pepper

3 1/2 oz salt

1 tsp ground white pepper

1 1/2 oz powdered dextrose

1 tsp ground celery seed

6 oz fermento

Processing:

Cut the meat into small pieces, spread on a plastic-covered cookie sheet and place in the freezer for 20 minutes. Remove and grind meat on a 1/8 inch grinder plate. Mix with the above ingredients to a uniform consistency, then stuff into an18 millimeter collagen casing.

Cut into uniform lengths of about 9 inches, line up on drying racks spaced slightly apart and place in the smoker.

Smoking:

Keep the smokehouse temperature between 98° –110° F., with dampers wide open. Smoke for about eight to 20 hours, depending on the flavor you aim to obtain. Then raise the temperature until the sausage reaches an internal temperature of 145° F.

Store your finished sausage in a dry room at 50°-55° F.

BLACK BEAR

Back around 1956, I was a chef in a summer resort hotel in the Laurentian mountains of Quebec. The previous fall, when they were ready to close for the winter, the European-born owners of the hotel heard that a neighboring farmer shot a huge black bear. Inquiring as to what he did with it, they were told he threw it on the dump. What else could he do with it? That was a common practice. They called the farmer and asked if he was willing to bring it over. For twenty dollars, he was very happy to do it. A butcher friend of theirs came, skinned and butchered the bear. They rendered the large amount of fat and stored it in gallon jars. The boneless meat was packaged and placed in ice cream cabinets outside on the porch, which eventually froze up and stopped working for the remainder of the cold Canadian winter.

When I arrived the following spring, the owners sheepishly told me about the bear meat and asked whether I would be willing to cook it for their guests. I had never previously cooked bear meat and was fully aware that it was totally illegal to serve. But I agreed to do it. After all,

I thought, how much different could it be from other wild game I cooked before? We called it "Hunters Pot Roast", made Goulash, etc. When customers asked, they were told it was beef. Some probably wondered. The taste was somewhat a cross between venison and pork.

Over the summer, I used up all of the bear meat without any problem. The lady of the house was a very good pastry cook and she baked various pastries using only the bear fat, which was kept in the walk-in cooler. The color of the fat was bright yellow and the pastries had a beautiful appearance, like full of egg yolks. To my amazement, they also tasted quite delicious! And I always thought that bear fat was only good for hunting boots!

BRAISED BLACK BEAR

with port wine and dried fruit

Note: I do not recommend cooking bear meat to medium rare because of possible parasites in the meat. The meat will take four to five hours of cooking time to get it tender.

3/4 cup unsalted butter, raw	1 oz Crème de Cassis
6-8 lbs trimmed meat	1/4 cup bacon fat
1 heaping Tbsp garlic	1 cup port wine
1/4 cup lemon juice	2 cups brown pork or veal stock
1/2 cup olive oil	1/4 cup sweet Vermouth
1/2 medium-sized onion, sliced	1 oz dark rum
1 branch celery, sliced	1 oz Crème de Cassis
1 small carrot, sliced	2 strips lemon zest
1 parsley root, sliced	2 strips orange zest
10 allspice berries	4 Tbsp arrowroot (or corn starch)
2 Tbsp black peppercorns	1/4 cup sweet Vermouth
8 bay leaves	1 oz dark rum
20 juniper berries	

Bone a leg of black bear, trim excess fat and sinew, cut meat into suitable chunks. Rub the meat with garlic, lemon juice and oil. Mix spices and vegetables together, place a layer of the mixture in the bottom of a stainless, glass or plastic container, place meat in and cover with remaining spiced vegetables. Seal tightly, refrigerate. Let marinate for roughly three days, turning over daily.

To cook:

Clean vegetable-spice mix from meat. Reserve. Season meat with salt. Preheat a skillet and add bacon fat. Brown the meat on all sides and then transfer to a braising pan.

Add the marinade vegetables to the skillet and brown slightly. Squash pan with 1 cup port wine and the stock. Bring it to a boil, then pour everything over the meat.

Cover, place in 300° F. oven and braise, turning occasionally, until fork tender (about 3 ½ to 5 hours).

2 cups dried fruit: prunes, apricots, cherries, raisins
1 cup ruby port wine

To plump: place fruit in a small sauce pan, add port wine and bring to a boil. Remove from fire, cover and allow to steep.

Sauce:

Transfer meat to another dish, cover and keep warm. Strain the remaining juices into a saucepan; do not use aluminum pans at any time. If necessary, reduce juice by boiling to desired amount of sauce. Add zest. Bring to simmer. Mix arrowroot and Vermouth and thicken the sauce to a syrupy consistency only. Whip in butter and add rum and Cassis. Add plumped fruit. Taste and adjust as necessary.

To serve:

Slice meat, arrange on plates, and spoon sauce with fruit over. Serve with polenta and a salad.

ANOTHER BEAR STORY

Many years later, I was a guest invited to come bear hunting with a select group of hunters (one was a high ranking officer of GM who flew in on his private jet) in Manitoba. I got my bear the first day of hunting and had nothing to do for the rest of the week. I told everyone I wanted to take the meat home (the other hunters left theirs in the bush); they wondered why I would want it. The resort owner's wife became interested in the prospect and asked me if I would be willing to cook a bear meat dinner for everyone. I agreed. We kept it a secret and one afternoon I cooked the meat as a goulash. They served it, without saying a word. The guides who had a table in the dining room for themselves were served the same as the guests. After everyone cleaned their plates, the owner's wife came and asked how they liked it. They all agreed it was very good! Being told they ate bear dropped some chins. The guides thought it was moose and could not tell the difference.

BRAISED WILD BOAR WITH BLACK BEER

6-8 lbs trimmed meat	8 bay leaves
salt	2 Tbsp black peppercorns
1/4 cup bacon fat	3/4 cup unsalted butter, raw
1 heaping Tbsp garlic	2 cups dark beer
1 large onion, sliced	1 cup brown pork or veal stock
1 branch celery, sliced	2 strips lemon zest
1 small carrot, sliced	3 Tbsp corn starch
1 parsley root, sliced	4 Tbsp brandy
10 juniper berries	2 cups dried prunes plumped in ½ cup of dark beer
a large pinch thyme	

To cook:

Season meat with salt. Preheat a skillet and add bacon fat. Brown the meat on all sides and then transfer to a braising pan.

Add the vegetables and seasonings to the skillet and brown slightly. Squash pan with beer and the stock. Bring it to a boil and then pour everything over the meat.

Cover, place in 300° F. oven and braise, turning occasionally, until fork tender (about three to four hours).

Sauce:

Transfer meat to another dish, cover and keep warm. Strain the remaining juices into a saucepan; do not use aluminum pans at any time. If necessary, reduce juice by boiling to the desired amount of sauce. Add zest. Bring to a simmer. Mix starch with brandy and thicken the sauce to a syrupy consistency only. Add plumped prunes. Taste and adjust as necessary.

To serve:

Slice meat, arrange on plates, and spoon sauce with fruit over. Serve with polenta and a salad.

SECTION: SMALL GAME

In most European countries, the sport of hunting is very strictly regulated. Hunters must schedule their hunt in advance and be accompanied by a game warden. After the hunt, if the hunters want to keep any of the game (which is still considered state property), they must purchase it from the game warden. The rest of the game is then tagged and shipped on the next train to the city where it is sold in butcher shops.

Large game is first gutted while small game is sold whole, as is. The customer may elect to have the game plucked or skinned and gutted by the store staff. However, most will take it home to hang and age it first. In Europe, fresh game is not considered ready for cooking any more than freshly made wine or cheese is consumable.

As a boy growing up in Prague, I remember my dad occasionally bringing home a hare or wild ducks. In each case, after a brief inspection, a string was tied to their feet and then they were suspended outside our window on the second floor of our apartment building. Depending on the ambient outside temperature, they hung there one to three weeks. By that time, they turned green and blue and smelled quite ripe. Only then were they considered ready for cooking. My mother was an excellent cook and I, myself, at the age of nine years, already had a great interest in anything wild, and volunteered to pluck or skin and gut them. And when the cooking aroma filled the kitchen, I was just drooling and could hardly wait for the feast.

We were not poor and game was expensive, but for me there was no better food.

Years later, as a cook's apprentice, my prior experience came in handy, as it was my job to clean and prepare wild game. Working in a very expensive restaurant, I gained the opportunity to learn cooking of various game species. In the fall, we always had game hanging in the cooler, aging. On the way to work, I used to pass by a sporting goods store. In the window, they had pictures of American bowhunters with big game. I used to stand there for a long time, gazing at those pictures, dreaming if I ever could...

CARE OF SMALL GAME, UPLAND GAME BIRDS & WATERFOWL

Gamebirds and furred small game animals must be allowed to cool as rapidly as possible after being shot. However, I do not recommend field dressing gamebirds and small game animals on the spot. Gutting small game creates openings through which airborne bacteria will enter the body.

After arriving home, the game should either be hung, spread on a cold floor, or if the weather is too warm, placed in a refrigerator. Once I found a grouse in a paper bag I had forgotten in the refrigerator for about a month. It was still in perfect shape. That was the best grouse I ever ate!

In the garage, keep a window open for ventilation. In a reasonably cool (34°-45° F.) temperature, small game can be aged for two weeks or longer. Should an odor develop, do not be alarmed. And green or blue skin is normal and will assure a great tasting meal!

Badly gut-shot game will have to be used sooner, within three to four days. Only after aging, gamebirds should be plucked, but never skinned. Dipping them briefly in very hot water helps to loosen the feathers.

To marinate birds, use ½ cup of madeira or dry sherry wine per bird with a shot of brandy, about 1 cup total of carrots, onions and celery, also whole black pepper, thyme and bay leaf. The liquid should not cover the game. Ceramic or glass dishes are best for this, and you should keep the marinade tightly covered. Turn the meat over daily and in this state you can keep it for a week, refrigerated. Use the marinade liquid and vegetables in cooking the birds.

AGE SMALL GAME?

Just as with big game, aging tenderizes small game, upland game birds and waterfowl, and improves their flavor. It takes about three days for muscles to relax after rigor mortis sets in. Small game must be aged whole, un-gutted, as an opening would bring in airborne bacteria and start spoiling it. We hang hare, ducks and pheasants by their hind feet for two to three weeks. Only then should you pluck the feathers or pull off the hide and gut the animals. The flesh will turn blue and green and there will be an odor which will completely dissipate during cooking. Anyone who has tasted aged small game will testify to the great flavor they acquire through aging.

To freeze small game, tightly wrap it in plastic to keep air out. Ducks freeze best when left whole, with feathers on. Cleaned ducks can be placed in half-gallon milk cartons filled with water. Cleaned wild ducks, dry frozen will turn rancid when kept for more than two months. Aged pheasants can be frozen in vacuum-packed heavy plastic bags.

DUCK

There are many species of wild duck. For cooking, we break them down into roughly two main groups: puddle ducks (mallards, blacks, canvasbacks, teal, etc.) and diving ducks (bluebills, mud hens, etc.). The latter group feeds mainly on fish. Avoid the fish-eating ducks, since they have a bad taste and odor.

BRAISED WILD DUCK OR GOOSE

4 servings

Before braising your birds, take care that all feathers are removed, because they give off an unpleasant odor. You can cut off the last section of the wings and discard it, but the skin of the birds should not be removed, as it protects them from drying out during cooking.

2 large or 4 small ducks (or 1 medium-sized goose)	1/4 cup cooking oil
coarse salt	1 medium carrot, coarsely cut
8 bay leaves	1 medium onion, coarsely cut
1/4 cup peppercorns	1 cup dry red burgundy
1 tsp leaf thyme	1 cup brown veal stock or 2 bouillon cubes and water
4 whole allspice	1/2 tsp powdered arrowroot or corn starch
1 apple, quartered	1 heaping Tbsp raw butter
2 branches celery, snapped in half	

Preheat oven to 400° F. Rub the ducks inside and out with salt. Place a roasting pan, large enough to accommodate the birds without crowding, in the oven to preheat. Place the herbs, spices, celery and apple inside the ducks, dividing evenly, and then tie them with a string. Pour oil into the heated roasting pan and place the ducks in, breast side up. Brown for about 20 minutes on all sides.

Lower the oven temperature to 325° F. Add the chopped onion and carrot to the pan, turn the birds breast side down, cover and cook for 20 minutes. Then add half the wine and half the stock, and continue braising, pan covered, turning occasionally and adding liquid as needed until the birds are done, or for approximately an hour and a half (goose may take 3-4 hrs). Should the liquid evaporate, add a little water. To test for doneness, pinch the drumsticks with your fingers.

Transfer the cooked birds to a baking sheet, and cover to keep them warm. Strain the juice from the pan into a small saucepan.

Carefully skim off all fat and discard. If more than 1/2 cup juice remains, boil it down. Dissolve the arrowroot in about 2 Tbsp more wine or water, and add the mixture to the juice to thicken it. Bring to boil again, and then remove from fire, adding the raw butter.

Taste and correct seasoning if necessary.

Before serving, split birds in half lengthwise, remove spine, wish bones and rib cage, place the halves skin side up in a pan, crisp skin for a few minutes in a 500° F oven.

ROAST WILD DUCK

4 servings

2 full-sized ducks (or 4 small ones)	2 bay leaves
coarse salt	a pinch of thyme
pepper	melted butter or oil

For best results, cut the legs off and braise them to tender in advance (directions in preceding recipe). Instead of roasting them, sear the legs in a skillet, and then add the vegetables and liquids. Braise them covered on low heat. Make the sauce from cooking the legs.

To roast the breasts: Preheat oven to 450° F. Also preheat a heavy skillet.

Season the breasts inside and out with salt and pepper. Put the rest of the seasonings inside. Pour a little oil into the heated skillet, add the breasts and sear them to brown all around. Then place the pan in the oven, for about 10 minutes, depending on their size. They have to remain rare.

Remove the breasts from the pan and keep warm. Allow them to rest 10-15 minutes.

In the meanwhile, reheat the legs in the sauce. To serve, slice the rare breasts lengthwise into very thin slices, place a leg on a plate and drape the breast slices over.

Cooking it to well-done will result in a very tough bird.

Serve with potato pancakes, braised red cabbage or Chinese stir-fried vegetables.

WILD DUCK WITH ORANGE SAUCE

Braise the ducks as per the instructions given in braised duck recipe, using a dry white wine or vermouth in place of red wine. For the sauce:

6 oranges	1/3 cup lemon juice
4 Tbsp sugar	1 Tbsp arrowroot or corn starch
4 tsp vinegar	

Using a peeler, thinly peel the rind of two oranges into strips; cut these into a fine julienne and boil them in water for two minutes and then drain, rinse and set them aside.

Completely remove the peel of three oranges and section them. Set aside.

Place the sugar in a small saucepan and, with a touch of water, melt it to golden brown. Add vinegar and boil up. Set aside.

Strain the juices from the roasting pan – the duck drippings – through a fine mesh strainer. Add the sugar/vinegar. Squeeze the juice of the remaining oranges and add it, together with the lemon juice, to the sauce. Boil it, cooking the mixture down to 3/4 cup. Lightly thicken it with arrowroot mixed with a little water and finish with butter, as in the previous recipe. Add julienne of orange peel to the sauce. When serving, garnish ducks with orange sections, and pour the sauce over all.

Serve with wild rice pilaf, red cabbage or potato pancakes.

STEAK OF WILD DUCK

4 servings

The breasts of 2-4 ducks	pepper
salt	3 Tbsp vegetable oil

Cut the legs and wings off the ducks, reserving them for other uses. Bone the breast starting on top along the ridge of the breast bone and proceeding down the bottom. Peel the skin off. You should now have two steak-size fillets from each duck.

Preheat a large heavy skillet to smoking hot. Season the steaks on both sides with salt and pepper. Pour oil into skillet and place the steaks in it immediately.

Cook for about one minute on each side of the fillet, either over high heat or to rare doneness. Transfer to a warm platter. Pour off any grease from the skillet and swirl in the cognac and veal stock. Reduce to 1/3 cup by rapid boiling. Add peppercorns. Stir in the raw butter and pour the resulting sauce over the steaks.

These steaks can also be grilled. Simply preheat the grill to hot, put a little oil on the steaks and grill to rare as you would any other steak. Cooking the breast to well-done will result in a very tough dish. Omit the sauce.

Suggested accompaniments: potatoes, vegetables, salads or wild mushrooms.

STIR-FRIED DUCK OR PHEASANT BREASTS

with Pea Pods, Scallions and Mushrooms
4 servings

The recipe uses only the breasts of the birds. The legs need not be wasted, however, and you can braise them or use in a confit.

Breasts of 4 mallards or 2-3 pheasants, boneless and skinless, cut into 1/2 inch slices across the grain

3 Tbsp peanut or other vegetable oil	1 garlic clove, mashed
2 cups pea pods, stems pinched off	1/4 cup soy sauce
1 cup scallions cut into 1inch long pieces	2 Tbsp corn starch mixed with 3 Tbsp sherry wine
2 cups sliced mushrooms	a pinch of cayenne pepper or a few dashes of Tabasco
2 Tbsp grated fresh ginger root	

Preheat a large skillet, two medium-sized ones or a wok to smoking hot. Add the oil and spread the meat on the bottom in one layer without crowding. If you have more meat than will fit, prepare it in two batches. Over high heat, brown the meat on one side, and then turn it over and brown the other side. This should take about 15-20 seconds, and the meat should remain rare.

Remove the meat to another dish, add the vegetables, garlic and ginger to the skillet.

Add a little more oil if necessary. Stir-fry the vegetables until they reach a vibrant color and are heated through. Do not cook them, they should remain crisp.

Add the soy sauce and the sherry-starch mix, and stir it up. Season with cayenne, return the meat to the pan, fold it in and serve immediately over rice or noodles, or with crusty bread.

CONFIT

This dish is prepared primarily with domestic geese or ducks. However, it can be made with wild waterfowl, pheasant legs and venison shanks with very nice results. The name in French means "preserves". In days before refrigeration, country folks, both here and in Europe, used to preserve meat by salting it and then cooking it very slowly in fat. Completely immersed in fat, the meat was then stored in large crocks in cold cellars. This was done at the onset of winter and the meat thus preserved kept well for several months.

Even though the meats are cooked totally immersed in fat, once drained they are not at all greasy and make great warm or cold dishes. Apple horseradish is a nice garnish for cold or warm confit. The French baked bean dish called "cassoulet" is made with confit.

Whole birds will have to be quartered first. Legs should remain whole, and can be either skinned after cooking or skinless.

Mix together:

1/2 cups kosher salt	1 Tbsp crushed juniper berries
1/4 cup granulated sugar	1 tsp curing salt (nitrate)
2 qts duck, goose, pork or chicken fat (often found in Jewish delis) to cover.	

Sprinkle the meat pieces fairly heavily with the salt-sugar mixture on all sides. Wrap them in plastic, then place in a ceramic, glass or plastic container – not an aluminum one! Refrigerate for 24 hours. This cures the meat.

To cook:

Brush the salt mixture off the meat, but do not wash it off. Place meat in a large, heavy-bottomed pot and cover completely with melted fat. Bring it to a simmer on medium heat before reducing heat to very low and holding at 180°-200° F. Cook very slowly at this temperature until meat gets very tender. The cooking time will vary depending on the age of the animal. It may take up to 5+ hours.

Remove the meat from the fat, cover it and cool. If you want to reuse the fat, place it back on the fire and cook a little faster until all bubbles disappear. Strain and cool immediately.

To keep the meats for a longer time, place them back in the cooked fat, cool and refrigerate.

You can use confit as a cold dish, as a topping on pizza, served warm with grilled breast, shredded in salads or chopped on toast with a little sauce as an appetizer.

PHEASANT

While hunting pheasants with friends in South Dakota, after every hunt I hung my birds in the barn, letting them cool. Before leaving to go home, I placed them unmolested as they were, in a cooler. At home I hung them in my garage. My friends, to avoid plucking, pulled the skin off their pheasants, cut the wings and feet off and gutted them before leaving.

It is customary to have pheasants processed at a shooting preserve immediately after the hunt, while they are still in rigor mortis. If you want to produce an excellent dish, this is not advisable. Pheasant, as well as ducks and most small game need to be aged. I have described small game aging earlier in this book, so we do not need to revisit the subject. If you are willing to try it, you will be amazed at the difference aging makes.

It is customary for some hunters to clean their wild birds by skinning them, rather than plucking the feathers. Skinned pheasants are nearly impossible to roast to a juicy state. You may however braise, stew or stir-fry them, but don't expect great results.

To facilitate removal of feathers, you can dip the birds briefly in 180° F. water.

ROAST PHEASANT

6 servings

Immature pheasant (2 months old or less) can be roasted whole, in a 450° F oven for about 20 minutes. It will come out tender and juicy. But once the pheasant reaches maturity, its legs are tough from constant running. This is true even in farm raised pheasants. For best results, you need to cook the legs first, braising them for about 1½ hours (this can be done ahead of time) and roast the breasts before serving.

Ingredients:

3 pheasants

3 Tbsp bacon fat

1 onion, small, chopped

1 apple, small, chopped

2/3 cup game or veal stock

salt

1/2 cup dry Madeira

1 tsp thyme leaves

6 bay leaves

6 allspice berries

1 Tbsp arrowroot or corn starch

2 Tbsp water or stock

1 Tbsp cold butter

For breasts:

3 sheets thin-sliced back fat about 5x6 inches, or 6 strips of bacon

salt

game spice

string for tying

2 Tbsp clarified butter

Preheat oven to 325° F. Cut off legs and wings from breasts; split legs through back bone. Remove wishbones from breasts to facilitate carving. Season breasts with ground game spice; cover each with a sheet of fat or bacon strips and tie fat on with string. Place them in a refrigerator.

In a sautoir, sear legs and wings in bacon fat on both sides, remove; drain excess fat if necessary, add onion and apple, sauté until tender. Deglaze pan with wine and the stock, season legs and wings with salt, place back in sautoir, add rest of seasonings; bring to simmer on top of stove, cover and place in a 325° F oven.

Cook legs for approximately 1 ½ hours, or until tender; lift them out to another dish, keep covered. Strain pan juice into a small saucepan; discard wings and vegetable-spice residue; skim fat if excessive.

Dissolve the arrowroot in the water; pour this mixture into the juice, bring to boil, and taste to correct seasonings. Remove sauce from fire, whip butter in; keep warm.

To roast the breasts (35 minutes before serving time): preheat oven to 400° F.

Preheat a suitable skillet or roasting pan; pour butter in, place breasts in and sear on all sides. Transfer pan to preheated oven; roast for 20-25 minutes, depending on size. During this time, pull tendons out of drumsticks (needle nosed pliers work well), remove pelvic bone from legs; reheat legs in sauce, gently, without boiling.

Remove breasts from oven, allow to rest for five minutes. Drain fat from roast pan and deglaze the pan with sauce. Remove string from breasts; carve, thinly slicing parallel to breastbone.

To serve, place a leg on a plate and fan breast slices over one side of leg. Spoon sauce over.

CURRIED PHEASANT

6 servings

3 pheasants

salt to taste

3 cups plain yogurt

1 cup of coconut milk (canned)

1/2 cup clarified butter

1 qt onions, sliced

5 Tbsp imported Madras curry powder

1 large ripe banana, sliced

2 cups seedless green grapes

1 jar mango chutney

Cut off the wings and legs. Split drumsticks and thighs. Bone out the breasts and cut each into three pieces. Season the meat with salt and mix with yogurt and coconut milk. Cover and marinate for two hours. In a heavy, non-aluminum saucepan, sauté the onions in butter until they start to brown. Add the curry and sauté for a few more minutes.

Separate the breast meat from the rest and set it aside. Add the legs and wings to the onions, along with the yogurt, coconut milk and banana. Bring to a slow simmer, stir and cover. Simmer slowly, stirring once in a while, until legs get tender (about 1 ½ hours). Add the breasts, bring back to simmer, and cook for five minutes. Before serving, add the grapes. Serve over steamed rice with chutney on the side.

GROUSE

In North America alone, there are 18 species of grouse with size and flavor differences. The white-meated ruffed grouse, prairie chicken and sharp-tailed grouse can be treated the same as pheasant. These are the better tasting ones. The dark-meated western blue, spruce and sage grouse, as well as the various ptarmigans should be cooked within two days, as their meat will get progressively stronger tasting with age. The sage grouse has to be emptied as soon as possible after the kill to prevent the oil of the sage brush buds they feed on to permeate the meat with bitter results.

Likewise, the time it takes to cook the various grouse depends on their size. I prefer to keep the breast pink by the bone on white-meated birds and more rare on the dark-meated ones. Otherwise the various birds will be dry and tough. Same as with pheasants, the legs may need to be cooker longer to become tender. To determine the age of the grouse, lift it up by holding it by the lower beak. If it is a young bird, it will break. Also, a young bird's skull can be easily crushed with your thumb, and the two first wing feathers are pointed. Old birds are better suited for braising.

ROAST RUFFED GROUSE

with mushrooms & livers

4 serving

4 young grouse	1/2 cup celery, chopped
salt and ground game spice	1 cup brown stock
8 slices of bacon	1 cup fresh chicken livers
3 Tbsp clarified butter	1 1/2 cups sliced mushrooms
1/2 cup onion, chopped	1 tsp starch
1/2 cup carrot, chopped	1 Tbsp cognac

Preheat oven to 375° F. Season birds inside and out with salt and game spice. Cut bacon into halves, crosswise, and drape four halves over each breast. Attach with a cotton string.

Heat a roasting pan, add butter and the grouse and sear them quickly on all sides. Place pan in the oven, roast 10 minutes on one side, turn over and roast for five minutes on the other side. Then turn them breast-side up and roast for five more minutes.

Remove the grouse from the pan and allow to rest for 10 minutes. Then cut off the legs.

If too rare, return them to the oven for 5 more minutes. Cut the breast off the bone. Keep the meat covered and warm.

Chop the bones. Add them to the roasting pan, together with the vegetables. Over high heat, stir continuously to brown both. Add the wine, reduce a little, add the stock and simmer for 15 minutes. Strain, allow to settle, and skim off the fat.

While the sauce is simmering, preheat a skillet, add butter and over high heat quickly brown the livers while keeping them pink. Remove them using a slotted spoon and then add the mushrooms to the skillet. Cook these to limp, then add to the livers.

To serve, place the grouse back in the oven to reheat. It should remain pink! Bring the sauce back to a simmer, and thicken it by adding the starch mixed with the cognac. Then, add the livers and the mushrooms, and remove from fire.

Arrange the grouse on plates and spoon the sauce over them. Serve with brown rice, yam puree or cranberry relish.

PARTRIDGE

The smaller, grey so-called **Hungarian partridge** has exquisitely flavored dark meat. They also improve greatly by aging for a couple of weeks. Young birds are suitable for roasting, older ones for braising. **Chukkar partridge** yields white meat and can be handled as if they were small grouse. Young ones are roasted whole. The flavor is nutty and mild.

QUAIL

Quail provide good taste in small packages. We have six native species of quail in the U.S., ranging in size from three to 10 ounces in feather. This size difference must be taken into account during cooking. Age the birds whole, refrigerated, in a paper bag, for between four and five days, and then pluck and draw them. The hearts and livers are very good sautéed.

BOBWHITE QUAIL SAUTÉED WITH GRAPES

4 servings

8 quail, split open through the back, spine, ribs and wishbones removed

kosher salt	1/2 cup brown veal stock
pepper	1 cup seedless grapes
1/4 cup butter, melted	1 Tbsp butter
1 oz cognac	

Season the birds with kosher salt and pepper. Heat a large skillet to very hot. Pour in melted butter and place the quail in it. Over high heat, brown them nicely on both sides. Pour excess butter off, add cognac, and flame. Add veal stock and reduce the mixture down to about 1/4 cup of sauce.

Add grapes and 1 Tbsp butter; swirl around. As soon as grapes are heated, serve. The whole cooking time of the dish should not exceed 10 minutes.

GRILLED DOVE

Because of their small size and tiny legs, we generally use only the breasts of doves.

The best and easiest way to cook them is to cut the breast meat off the bone. At this point, you can marinate them using olive oil, garlic and herbs with a touch of brandy for a few hours before grilling. You can also use our Chinese marinade.

To facilitate grilling, skewer three or four breasts on bamboo or steel skewers, then grill them over very hot coals - to medium rare only! Overcooked breasts will be very tough. Season doves with salt and pepper before grilling.

Note: soak bamboo skewers in water for 2 hrs before grilling, to minimize burning.

Use two skewers, side by side for easier handling and to prevent meat from spinning around.

ROAST WOODCOCK WITH WILD MUSHROOMS

6 servings

In Europe, it is customary to leave the cleaned head of a bird on for cooking and serving. The neck is twisted back and the point of the bill is stabbed into the leg. The bird is then trussed, or tied with string, to ensure its shape. After roasting, the head is split in two lengthwise and placed in the center of the plate between the two breasts. Guests pluck out and eat the brain.

Woodcock should not be skinned if they are going to be roasted. Plucking such a small bird is very easy.

6 woodcock	2 qts wild mushrooms, cut into 1 inch pieces
4 Tbsp clarified butter	6 Tbsp clarified butter
salt	1 cup brown stock
pepper	3 Tbsp cognac
ground game spice	1 Tbsp lemon juice

Preheat oven to 425° F. Preheat a large skillet or roaster. Season the birds, pour butter into the hot pan, place the birds in and sear them quickly to golden brown on all sides. Place the pan in the oven to roast for eight minutes.

While the birds are in the oven, preheat another large skillet or shallow saucepan. Add butter and mushrooms and sauté until the mushrooms are heated through and became limp. Set them aside and keep warm and covered.

Remove the birds from the pan and allow them to rest for three minutes. Cut the breasts off the bone and keep warm and covered.

Chop the remaining carcasses and place them back in the roasting pan. Over high heat, brown them on top of the stove well, stirring. Add the stock, cognac and lemon juice. Scrape the sides and bottom of the pan, and then cook for five minutes. Strain, pressing out all the juices.

To serve, gently reheat the breasts in the juice, keeping them rare. Serve two breasts per plate, surrounded with mushrooms, sauce spooned over.

Serve with vegetable pancakes and pea pods.

GRILLED WOODCOCK

6 servings

Allow the whole birds to age for four to seven days. After this, skin and draw them.

6 woodcock	6 Tbsp olive oil
ground game spice	12 slices of bacon
6 Tbsp cognac	12 wetted toothpicks

Using a sharp knife, bone out the breasts starting at the ridge of the breast bone and continuing down around the rib cage. Place the breasts in a glass or ceramic dish, then season them with the spice, cognac and oil. Gently rub them together to coat evenly. Cover and refrigerate them for two hours – or overnight.

Prepare a hot bed of charcoal. Wrap each piece of breast in a slice of bacon, secure with wetted toothpick to prevent flaming, and grill for 30-40 seconds on each side, making sure the breasts remain rare. The bacon should be charred at this point. Serve immediately with grilled mushrooms, celeriac puree and a salad.

JERRY CHIAPPETTA'S DEEP-FRIED WILD TURKEY

When you're eating a deep-fried turkey, you don't carve the meat into slices. You tear it off in hunks, lick your fingers and gnaw on the bones. Deep fried wild turkeys are great!

The bird will come out of the deep-fryer very dark brown and crackling crisp on the outside, while the inside will remain white and succulent. With garlic oil and hot sauce, it's really spicy and delicious. When you deep-fry a wild turkey you'll have a special culinary treat as the culmination of your hunt, the ultimate enjoyment of your wild harvest. Deep-frying is especially good because it keeps the meat very moist and avoids overcooking. This recipe describes a technique for deep-frying an entire turkey that originated in Louisiana as a Cajun specialty.

The cooking is best done outside to prevent burning the house down. You may want to have fire extinguishers on hand. You'll need a deep cooking pot large enough to hold four gallons of peanut oil in addition to a whole turkey. Only oils with high smoke points should be used. These include peanut, canola and sunflower oils. The turkey must be clean, **dry** and plucked. Immersing a wet turkey in hot oil will result in explosion!

To fry, first heat peanut oil to 400° F, using a meat thermometer to check the temperature. Lower the turkey into the oil very slowly using a hook or wire, heavy gloves and wearing a heavy apron. Be extremely careful that the oil does not boil over and catch fire. If the peanut oil is hotter the turkey will cook crispier and faster. Move the turkey slowly and carefully once in a while. Leave the pot uncovered during cooking.

Peanut oil is best used within 30 to 90 days after the container has been opened. If the oil is to be re-used, it should be strained and filtered before storing. If you're using spices and herbs, it will be mandatory for the oil to be filtered through a fine cheesecloth to remove all of the residue imparted by them. The filtered oil should then be stored in a tightly-sealed container and placed in the refrigerator to prevent it from becoming rancid. Peanut oil and other oils with high smoke points can be used three to four times to deep-fry turkeys before deterioration. Such indications include foaming, darkening or smoking excessively. Other signs of deteriorated oil include a rancid smell and a failure to bubble when food is added. Check with authorities in your area for the proper way to dispose of the old oil. Most restaurants have an oil barrel in the back of the house.

The best way to season your turkey is with an injector and a spicy sauce. Use at least 1/2 oz. of sauce per pound of turkey, making sure to inject the sauce deeply and evenly.

Season with salt, black pepper, cayenne or red pepper, garlic powder, onion powder and celery salt. Much of the seasoning applied to the outside of the turkey will wash off during cooking, so don't be conservative when adding it. Season the turkey the night before in order to allow the seasoning to work better.

Deep-frying time ranges from three to five minutes per pound. Try cooking birds of 10 to 12 lbs around three minutes per pound and larger birds about five minutes per pound. Make sure that the bird is completely submerged in oil during cooking.

Bind the turkey legs together with wire. Use another strong wire to slowly and carefully lower the bird into the boiling peanut oil. This will sear it immediately and hold in all the juices.

Immediately adjust your flame or heat source down slightly and maintain a temperature between 350° and 375° F. The oil should be hot enough to bubble during frying, but not so hot that it burns.

Turn it carefully every 10 to 15 minutes. Let the turkey fry until the juices run clear when you insert a skewer into the breast. Check for doneness by removing the wire basket from the hot oil and cutting the meat to the bone at the thigh-hip joint where it is densest. The meat should look pink, but not raw.

Carefully remove the turkey from the hot oil and place it breast-down on a platter or pan lined with several thicknesses of paper. Let it drain for about five minutes, then turn turkey over to drain and cool for about 15 minutes more before slicing. Carve as you normally do and serve immediately.

ROAST SQUAB PIGEON

6 servings

A pigeon that has not left the nest yet is called "squab." They have dark flesh and are quite tender and tasty. Once they have begun to fly their breasts toughen, but the breasts are still usable for grilling, providing that you cook them to rare only. Well-done pigeon breast will be very tough! The legs are best suited for stock.

6 squabs	1/2 cup brown stock
2 Tbsp game spice	2 Tbsp cold butter
4 Tbsp cognac	salt and pepper
4 Tbsp olive oil	3 Tbsp clarified butter

Cut off the wings, necks and legs, and set them aside. Place the breasts in a ceramic or glass dish and sprinkle with the game spice, cognac and olive oil. Roll them around to coat them evenly, then cover them snugly with plastic wrap and refrigerate for a day or two.

Preheat oven to 400° F Chop up the wings, necks and legs, and with gizzards and hearts, place in a roasting pan. You may add some chicken backs and necks for richer flavor. Add 1/2 inch of water and set the pan in the oven to roast.

Stir the bones occasionally to turn over the ones that have browned. When all water evaporates and the bottom of the roaster browns, place the pan on the stove and add a cup of water and the brown stock. Cook, scraping pan and stirring bones until juice has reduced to 3/4 cup. Strain into a small pan. Season to taste with salt; whip in the cold butter. This is your sauce.

To roast the breasts, preheat the oven to 450° F 15 minutes before serving, remove the breasts from the dish and pat them dry with paper towels. With a small sharp knife remove the wishbones. Preheat a large skillet to smoking hot. Season the birds with salt and pepper, add clarified butter to the skillet, and place the breasts in. Over high heat sear to brown on all sides, then put them, with the skillet, in the oven for five minutes. The breasts must remain rare!

Remove them to a platter, cover loosely and allow them to rest for five minutes.

To serve: using a sharp, thin-bladed slicing knife, slice the breasts 1/8 inch thick, parallel to the breastbone. Spill a little sauce on warm plates and arrange the slices over in a fan shape.

Serve with sautéed potatoes, yam puree, or wild rice and a nice vegetable such as pea pods, asparagus, or fresh green peas. Serve with a nice, light red wine.

SECTION: RABBITS AND SQUIRRELS

I prefer to leave rabbits and hare intact after shooting, allowing them to cool down fast. Upon arrival home, I either leave them in a cool garage or refrigerate them for about a week, unless gut-shot, in which case I keep them for a much shorter time. Only then are they skinned, drawn and washed.

The age of rabbits, hare and squirrels can be determined by size, tenderness of ears (very cartilaginous in young animals) and claw development. The hair on a well-fed animal is shiny.

Squirrels are prepared in the same way as cottontail rabbits. Both are sweet-tasting and can be cooked similar to domestic rabbits or even chicken. Snowshoe hare is much stronger tasting and is better prepared with a rich sauce or in a pâté.

After short aging, rabbits and other such small game animals are skinned, gutted and rinsed. You can further delay the cooking time of furred game by marinating it in 1 cup of dry white wine with root vegetables, herbs and spices. It can then be frozen or kept refrigerated for up to a week longer.

BRAISED COTTONTAIL RABBIT OR SQUIRREL

1 rabbit or 2 squirrels

salt, pepper

a pinch of thyme

1 bay leaf, crushed

12 small walnut-sized onions

3 Tbsp clarified butter

1/2 lb of firm white mushrooms

1/4 cup dry white wine

1/4 cup veal or chicken stock

Cut off the legs. Cut the remaining back into three even pieces. Season the meat with salt, pepper, thyme and bay leaf, and then set aside.

In a large heavy skillet, brown the onions gently in butter. Add mushrooms and sauté until limp. Remove both with slotted spoon.

To the skillet add the meat pieces and brown them nicely on all sides. Add wine and stock and lower heat to barely a simmer. Cover and place in 350° F oven for 1 to 1 ½ hours, or until tender. Should all liquid evaporate during cooking, add a little more broth. There should be about 4 Tbsp of sauce left when done. Add onions and mushrooms and cook for ten minutes more.

Suggested accompaniments: potatoes, black bean cakes, vegetable pancakes, wild mushroom strudel, streamed rice, celeriac puree or simple green vegetables.

JACK RABBIT – ANYONE INTERESTED?

While pheasant hunting in South Dakota, a jack rabbit sprung up and took off. Instinctively I swung my gun and shot it. Then I picked it up and placed it in my back pouch. A couple of my buddies looked at me with surprised looks and one said "what will you do with THAT?" Apparently, there is a rumor that jacks are not edible. When I asked why, no reason was given. After arriving back home, I hung it in the garage for a while, then took it to work with me. It was quite meaty and the loins yielded nice, thick medallions. After grilling them to medium rare I found them quite delicious. I braised the rest to tender and it was likewise very good to eat. So, who said you cannot eat them?

ROAST SNOWSHOE HARE WITH SOUR CREAM SAUCE

4 servings

1 snowshoe hare	1 cup dry white wine
1 medium onion	salt
4 whole allspice berries	1/4 lb thick sliced bacon
1 medium carrot	1/4 cup clear butter
1/2 small root celery (or two celery branches)	1 Tbsp flour
2 bay leaves	1 tsp prepared mustard
a pinch thyme	1 1/2 cup sour cream
20 whole peppercorns	4 heaping Tbsp lingonberries
1/2 lemon rind (peeled off thinly)	4 thin slices of lemon

Cut the thin belly and chest flanking off and discard. Split the pelvic bone between the hind legs. Holding the legs in your hands, with your thumbs resting on the hare's back, pull legs back to break them at the spine. This will allow the hare to lay flat during roasting.

Mix the vegetables with the spices and lemon peel. Place a layer of vegetables on the bottom of a deep oblong china, glass or stainless dish. Set the hare on this and cover with the rest of the vegetables. Pour in the wine and cover tightly. Refrigerate, turning hare in marinade occasionally, for a day or two.

Preheat the oven to 450° F. Lift the hare out of the marinade and pick off any spices or vegetables clinging to it. Pat dry with paper towel and season with salt. Place the hare in a roasting pan and cover with bacon slices and pour the butter over it. Place it in the oven and brown on all sides. Add marinating vegetables, spices and a little of the liquid. Cover the hare and lower the temperature to 325° F. Roast, turning once in a while, until tender, or for about 1 ½ hours. Add remaining marinade liquid if necessary. Transfer the hare to another dish and keep warm.

Place the vegetables in a sauce pan, add any remaining marinating liquid to it. Using a whisk, whip flour and mustard into sour cream to a smooth consistency. Add it to the vegetables, bring to a simmer and cook while stirring for 5 minutes. Strain, rubbing vegetables through a fine strainer. Taste the sauce and adjust the seasoning if necessary.

Cut the hare into serving pieces, place on plates. Spoon the sauce over. Heap lingonberries onto lemon slices and set on top of the hare. Suggested accompaniments: spaetzles, noodles, red cabbage, zucchini boats or cranberry relish.

WHAT ABOUT THE OTHER CRITTERS?

Over the years, I have had the opportunity to sample a good variety of wild animals, including African plains game. Those tasted pretty much all the same. They were always cooked quite well done. I suppose they were worried about parasites. Grilled items were not offered, which could have been very good.

Of our local fauna, I found beaver to be excellent, muskrats okay, raccoon too strong and musky tasting. I have never tried opossum. In Quebec I was curious about porcupines. They used to be protected, for the reason that a lost, starving hunter or fisherman could find them easy prey to catch. So I brought a big one to my future wife's mother and asked her if she would cook it for me. She agreed, with the condition that I would skin it, which proved a little difficult. It required welder's gloves and a pair of pliers to pull the slit skin apart.

I tasted the cooked meat and had to spit it out! It tasted like a rabbit sprinkled with turpentine. The reason? Commercially produced turpentine is extracted from pine bark and that is all the porcupines eat, circumcising and destroying the pines in the process.

From the venison type meats, moose, elk, caribou and whitetails are similar, but need to be aged. Antelope tends to have a strong tasting dark meat, from feeding on sage brush. Mule deer are not great eating, tough and strong, even when aged.

An item altogether different were small pieces of cougar served to us by a guide in Montana. It looked and tasted like rich veal. I liked it a lot!

SECTION: SIDE DISHES

CARBOHYDRATES

Spaetzle

A soft noodle dough dumpling. Its origin is sometimes disputed, but the dish likely came from Switzerland or Hungary.

3 eggs	salt
1/3 cup milk	nutmeg
1 cup semolina flour	chopped parsley
1 cup all-purpose flour	variation: add chopped fresh sage, chives or thyme.

Use either a spaetzle machine or large-holed colander. Bring a good amount of water to boil. Mix all ingredients together until smooth. Place the colander over boiling water (or fill the spaetzle machine) and push the dough into the water. Boil for two minutes and drain.

Shock with cold water and drain again. To serve, sauté spaetzle in clarified butter or vegetable oil until lightly browned.

Polenta

This traditional Italian dish has become popular in America. It has great versatility.

6 1/2 cups water

salt

2 cups coarse yellow cornmeal

Bring the water with salt to a boil and add the cornmeal in a very slow, steady stream, stirring constantly to prevent the formation of lumps.

Simmer, stirring, for about 20 minutes, or until the cornmeal pulls away from the sides of the pot.

This is the basic stuff. At this point, you can embellish it by adding one or several of the following: Butter, cream, freshly grated cheese (Parmesan, Romano, Gorgonzola, Asiago or other), chopped herbs, dried fruits and nuts.

If not served immediately, mold the polenta by pouring into (plastic wrap lined) rectangular molds and allowing it to set up. When cold, polenta can be cut into various shapes and reheated by sautéing, steaming or even grilling it. It makes an interesting side dish for game and other meat or poultry dishes.

Dumplings

1 egg

1/4 cup milk

1 cup all-purpose flour

2 Tbsp chopped parsley

1 tsp salt

1 tsp baking powder

flour for rolling

Mix egg and milk, add dry ingredients and parsley and mix to a smooth paste.

In a large pot, bring two quarts of water to a boil. Roll dough into strands 1inch thick and then cut into 1inch cubes. In your hands, roll each cube into a smooth ball. Drop the balls into the boiling water. Cook for five minutes, turning over once. Drain and prick dumplings with a fork to release steam. Dumplings can also be cooked in various creamed dishes and stews, floating them in the gravy.

If you make dumplings in advance, keep them covered so they do not develop a tough skin. To re-heat, place in a strainer over a pot with a little boiling water, cover and steam them.

Egg Noodles

You may wonder: why would anyone go to the extra effort to make their own noodles, when they can buy them (sometimes even fresh) in a store? It all depends on how discriminate your taste buds are. There are basically two types of pasta: *rolled* and *extruded*. There is a great difference in quality between the two.

Factory made pasta is *extruded*. That means a dry, meal consistency material made with dried eggs and perhaps milk powder and other substances mixed with flour is fed into very powerful machines, which compress the material into a solid consistency and extrude it through various shape dies, depending on the type of pasta desired. At that point the pasta is relatively dry and does not stick together. Obviously, it does not have the same fresh egg content of *rolled* pasta. As a result, during cooking it absorbs more water, making it mushy and slimy.

Quality restaurants make their own rolled pasta.

The following is a basic noodle dough recipe from which various types of rolled noodles, in addition to lasagna, ravioli and tortellini, can be made.

4 whole extra-large eggs

4 tsp of olive oil

2 cups semolina flour

approx. 2 cups unbleached all-purpose flour

Combine all ingredients into a smooth, very stiff dough. Cover it with inverted bowl and allow to rest in a cool place for an hour. After that, cut the dough into slices. Either use a noodle machine (recommended) or roll the dough out on a floured board to paper thinness. Hang the sheets of dough either over wood dowels, or place them on wooden boards, paper lined trays or large sheets of cardboard, without overlapping. Allow the sheets to dry only to a leathery consistency (15-20 min) before cutting them into noodles. Either drape the strands of noodles again over wooden dowels suspended between chairs or scatter them on boards, paper lined trays or even cardboard to dry overnight. When completely dry, store the noodles in cloth bags to allow them to *breathe*. Storing them in tightly closed containers may result in mold or rancidity. For lasagna and ravioli, the dough is rolled and used immediately.

To cook the noodles (fresh or dried), drop them into plenty of boiling, salted water. Cook them for about four minutes, then drain and serve. You may cook them in advance, drain, chill with cold water, drain again, cover and later reheat for service. You will find no difference between your cooked fresh or dried noodles, but a great difference between yours and store bought.

Fettuccine Alfredo

2 1/4 cups cooked fettuccine noodles   1/2 cup heavy cream

2 Tbsp butter

1/3 cup grated Parmesan (grating the cheese yourself will also make a big difference)

Cook the fettuccine in salted water and drain. In a skillet bring the rest of the ingredients to simmer, add the hot pasta, toss well and serve.

Black Bean Cakes

Serve these as an interesting complement to wild boar, bison or bear.

Soak black beans in water overnight. Cook them in an unsalted herbed stock until tender. Drain and coarsely mash them; add chopped jalapeno peppers, sliced scallions, crumbled bacon and a raw egg or two. Season with salt. Scoop out little balls, drop them into breadcrumbs and flatten into small cakes. Pan-fry them in clarified butter or bacon fat until crisp on both sides and heated through.

P.S. You may use canned black beans.

Potato Pancakes

Serve these with boar, bison, bear or ducks.

2 large Idaho potatoes, peeled and grated coarsely	2 eggs
4 Tbsp onion, grated finely	pinch of black pepper, marjoram
1 clove garlic, grated finely	clarified butter

Very important: This mixture must be used immediately when made; leaving it stand for more than 10 minutes will cause it to liquefy and become useless.

Mix all together. Drop spoonfuls into a hot pan containing clarified butter, flatten a little into cakes and brown on both sides. Stir the mixture well each time you dip the spoon in. Do not drain off any liquid. Place pancakes on paper towel-lined trays, season with salt. They can be made ahead of time (same day) and reheated in the oven for serving.

Byron Potatoes

Do not wrap potatoes for baking in foil. They will steam, rather than bake and will not taste great. You may instead grease them lightly with oil and season them with salt and pepper.

Take six large baked potatoes, split them in halves and scoop out the flesh. Break the flesh up into lumps, mix with 1/4 cup of butter, season it with salt and freshly ground pepper. Pack the mixture into a Pyrex, ceramic or stainless baking dish, level off and top with

1/2 cup of heavy cream. Let it sit for about ½ hour.

Preheat oven to 375° F. Sprinkle top of potatoes with 3/4 cup grated Gruyere or Swiss cheese and then place it in the oven and bake to golden brown.

For different appearance, you may fill the empty potato skins with the creamed mixture, top with cheese and bake. For a variation, add chopped ham and chives.

Anna Potatoes

4 large potatoes, peeled

1/2 cup clarified butter

salt

You will need a skillet that measures 10 inches across by 2 inches deep and is oven safe.

Preheat oven to 400° F.

Peel and thinly slice the potatoes crossways. Start lining up potato slices around the perimeter of the skillet, overlapping them in circles until the bottom is covered. Cover with another layer, but keep the surface flat. Pour the butter in the pan.

Place the pan on high heat to brown the bottom layer. Shake the pan occasionally to prevent potatoes from sticking and burning, but do not disturb the circles.

When the bottom layer has browned, set the skillet in the pre-heated oven to finish cooking. Cook for about 15- 20 minutes.

After removing it from the oven, cover the skillet with a lid, leaving a small opening at the edge, then tilt the pan sharply to drain all the butter off. Replace the lid with an upside-down platter and invert the pan quickly to unmold the potatoes. Sprinkle lightly with salt, serve immediately.

RICE

White rice is polished brown rice. There are several types of white rice available, and each has a different property. Use short grain for puddings and thickening, long grain for side dishes and Arborio rice for risotto. One of the best long grains is the imported Indian Basmati, harvested in the foothills of the Himalayas, in a disputed territory between India and Pakistan. The workers are often shot at and have to be guarded by armed soldiers.

You should always wash long grain rice before cooking. During shipment the grains rub against each other, creating rice starch. This starch, when not washed away, will cause the rice to become sticky.

Converted Rice - has been partially steamed and dried again. It doesn't need to be washed and is guaranteed to come out fluffy. But it has a slightly gluey taste.

Instant Rice: also has been pre-cooked and will save you just a few meaningless minutes. It has a very mediocre taste and texture.

Brown Rice is whole grain. It should be well washed before cooking.

Wild Rice is actually not a true rice, but the seeds of a grass that grows in water. In the old days, American and Canadian Indians harvested wild rice by paddling canoes into marshes, bending the wild rice stems over the canoes and beating the grains loose from the seed pods. Most of the wild rice on the market today is commercially cultivated in various states and Canada. It comes in several grades according to size, the "Giant Canadian" being the best. Broken rice is least expensive. Wild rice *"blends"* are a very poor choice. If you would count the grains, they would amount to about 30-50 grains of white rice to each grain of small wild rice. Since wild rice takes about five times longer to cook than white rice, the blend has been separately pre-cooked and dried again, resulting in what is called "converted" rice.

I call it perverted.

Steamed White Rice

An accompaniment suitable for many dishes.

2 cups long grain rice	1 small onion, studded with
2 Tbsp butter	1 whole clove
3 ½ cups water	1 tsp salt

In a mesh strainer, wash the rice, rubbing it gently until the water runs clear. Drain well. Bring water, butter and the rest of the ingredients to a boil, add the rice, stir, bring back to boil and stir for the last time.

Reduce the heat to a **very** low simmer, cover the pot tightly, and cook for 18 minutes **without peeking in**. Turn heat off and let the rice steam for two minutes more. **Only then** you may lift the cover off, remove the onion and stir the rice, using a kitchen fork. Serve immediately. White rice does not reheat well.

Greek (or Armenian?) Rice Pilaf

1 cup long grain rice	2 1/2 cups chicken broth
3 Tbsp clarified butter	1/2 bay leaf
1/2 cup onion, chopped finely	salt and white pepper to taste.
1 cup fine egg noodles or vermicelli (uncooked)	

In a strainer, wash the rice under cold water, rubbing gently until the water runs clear. Leave to drip dry.

In a heavy-bottomed saucepan heat the butter, then add the noodles. Stirring constantly, brown them evenly to a golden brown. Immediately add the onion and stir, cooking the onion to translucent only. Add the rice, stirring to coat the grains, and add the rest of the ingredients. Bring to a boil, stir again, lower the heat to **very** low, cover with a tight-fitting lid and mark the time.

Cook, without removing the lid, for 18 minutes. Turn the heat off and allow to stand for two more minutes. Remove the lid and the bay leaf and stir, using a kitchen fork to loosen the pilaf. Serve immediately.

Brown Rice with Raisins & Pecans

1 cup brown rice

1 Tbsp olive oil

2 cups chicken broth

1 tsp salt

1 tsp grated orange peel

1/3 cup pecan pieces, toasted

1/4 cup raisins

Preheat the oven to 325° F.

Wash the rice under running water and drain. Bring the oil, broth, raisins and salt to a boil in a heavy saucepan. Add rice, stir, cover tightly and place in the oven for one hour. Or, you may also cook it on top of the stove, similar to pilaf.

Toast the pecans on a sheet pan in same oven. When the rice is done, stir in the pecans and orange peel.

Wild Rice Pilaf

yields 3 cups

1 cup wild rice	1 bay leaf
3 Tbsp chopped bacon or ham	a pinch of thyme
1 Tbsp butter	1/4 cup onion, finely chopped
salt	1 cup wild rice
2 cups chicken stock	

Wash the rice and drain. Set aside. In a small saucepan sauté the bacon in butter until it starts to brown, add vegetables and cook to translucent, add rice, and stir well. Add stock and seasoning. Bring all to a boil, stir, cover and cook over low heat, stirring once in a while, until rice is tender (or for about 1 ½ hours). Add more stock if needed.

The rice will be done when it has fully expanded. Before serving, you can further enhance the flavor by adding toasted slivered almonds and chopped parsley or chives. Wild rice can be cooked in advance and reheated for serving.

Wild Rice, Celeriac & Parsnip Pancakes

Batter:

1 egg yolk	1 egg white
1 cup buttermilk	1/2 tsp salt
1 cup flour	1 tsp sugar
1/2 tsp baking powder	2 Tbsp melted butter

In a bowl, mix the egg yolk with buttermilk. Sift the flour with baking powder and mix in until smooth. Whip egg white with salt, adding sugar as done for a meringue. Fold this into the batter. Last, fold in the butter.

Use this basic batter as a binder for various vegetable pancakes.

For wild rice pancakes, add cooked wild rice, sliced scallions, crumbled bacon and toasted slivered almonds. For celeriac, parsnip and other vegetable pancakes, add a small amount of pancake mix to peeled, coarsely-grated raw vegetables.

Cook all vegetable pancakes in clarified butter in a medium-hot skillet to brown on both sides.

Remove to a sheet pan. You may need to finish cooking them through in a 325° F. oven. The size of the cakes should be very small, about 2-3 inches in diameter.

VEGETABLES

Roasted Vegetables

Preheat the oven to 400° F.

You may roast carrots, parsnips, root celery, asparagus, kohlrabi, onions, celery, bulb fennel, yams, Brussel's sprouts, cauliflower, broccoli, etc. Some need to be peeled first. Cut vegetables into finger size pieces. Season lightly with salt and dried thyme, toss with a small amount of olive oil.

Line the vegetables up on a sheet pan and roast them, turning occasionally, until they are soft. Roasted root vegetables are very flavorful and an excellent accompaniment with steaks, roasts and chops.

Stir-fried Vegetables

4 servings

For really great tasting stir fry, buy all fresh vegetables. Fresh water chestnuts (sold in Chinese groceries) taste far better than canned, same for bean sprouts and mushrooms.

You'll need 4-5 cups altogether of the following fresh vegetables mixed together:

scallions	pea pods or sugar snap peas
mushrooms	bean sprouts
bok-choy	water chestnuts

(other possible choices: carrots, zucchini, asparagus, broccoli, red peppers, kohlrabi, celery)

2 Tbsp peanut oil	1 tsp mashed garlic
1 Tbsp grated fresh ginger	2 Tbsp soy sauce

Wash the vegetables, mushrooms, etc. and peel them if needed. Cut mushrooms, zucchini and water chestnuts into ¼ inch thick slices, carrots and kohlrabi thinly, asparagus, peppers and bok-choy into bite size pieces, leave pea pods or sugar/ snap peas whole. Start with mushrooms, then add the rest and sauté the vegetables briskly in hot peanut oil – just heating through, not browning. Last, stir in the ginger and garlic. When the vegetables turn vibrant in color, they are done. Do not cook them! Season with soy sauce. You do not need to add salt, as the soy sauce is salty enough. You may wish to add some cayenne pepper though.

Brussels Sprouts with Bacon & Onions

Very good with grilled game, roasts and dishes without heavy or creamy sauces.

Clean the sprouts and trim the stem ends off. Leave the small ones whole, cutting an "X" in the stem, and split larger ones in half. Cook them in a stainless pot in salted water to al dente and drain. If you are not going to serve them immediately, shock them in cold water and drain again.

Cut the bacon crossways into ¼ inch pieces and in a skillet, cook with a little butter until lightly brown. Add sliced onion and cook until the onion starts to color. Season with marjoram and black pepper, add the sprouts and toss all together. You may reheat the sprouts later.

Roasted Tomatoes

Plum tomatoes are best for this preparation.

Preheat oven to 400° F.

Split the tomatoes lengthwise and remove the seeds and jellied juice. Sprinkle a little salt on them. Place them on an oiled sheet pan cut-side up and roast them, checking periodically, for about an hour, or until they lose about 60% of their water content.

Serve them as a vegetable or cut them up to add to pasta dishes. For an appetizer, place them on toast, add some sliced cheese topped with half-cooked bacon slices and bake.

Buttered Savoy Cabbage

While this is a very simple vegetable preparation, the cabbage has a nice, delicate flavor and makes a great accompaniment to grouse, woodcock, quail and pheasant.

1 small head of savoy (curly) cabbage	1/4 cup heavy cream
salt	1/3 cup softened butter

Split, core and cut the cabbage into 1 inch squares. In a stainless pot, bring some salted water to boil. Drop the cabbage in, stir, cover and cook briefly to al dente. Drain well.

In a large skillet, bring the cream to a boil. While whipping steadily with a wire whisk, start slowly adding the butter. When all butter is incorporated, add it to the cabbage and toss to coat evenly. Serve immediately.

Braised Red Cabbage

1 small head of red cabbage	garlic (optional)
¼ lb bacon, finely julienned	1 1/2 cups white wine, dry or medium
2 Tbsp butter	1/2 cup rich roast stock or reduced chicken stock
1 onion, sliced fine	pinch of salt
1 apple, julienned	pinch of thyme
3 bay leaves	

Remove the outer leaves of the cabbage. Core and slice it into ¼ inch strips.

Sauté bacon in butter until it starts to color. Add onion and sauté until translucent. Add the cabbage, apple, seasonings, stock and white wine.

Simmer, stirring occasionally, for about 30 minutes, or until the cabbage is tender. The amount of juice at this point should be minimal. If there is too much, reduce it by rapid boiling.

If the cabbage is to be reheated – it always tastes better the next day – leave it as is. Always taste and adjust seasoning (you may like to add a touch of vinegar or a pinch of sugar).

Yam Puree

(6 servings)

2 large or 3 medium yams	1/2 Tbsp lemon juice
3 Tbsp butter, melted	2 Tbsp heavy cream
1 Tbsp dark rum	1/2 tsp orange zest, grated

Bake the yams in 325° F oven for an hour, or until soft. Then cut them in halves, lengthwise, and scoop out the pulp. Put the pulp, along with the rest of the ingredients, into a processor and puree until smooth. Serve warm.

Note: the amount of all ingredients is relative to the size of the yams, and should be adjusted accordingly.

Root Celery (Celeriac) Puree

The root celery is a cousin of "regular" celery. It is sold in fall and winter, and looks like coarse-skinned turnips. It can be eaten raw, with mustard-flavored sour cream, or cooked and served as a salad with vinaigrette dressing. It makes an excellent garnish to various wild game dishes, especially venison.

3 large or 6 small roots	1 Tbsp lemon juice
1 medium-sized potato	salt and white pepper to taste
1 Tbsp sugar	3-4 Tbsp softened butter

Peel the roots and the potato, cutting them into quarters. Boil in salted water until tender. Drain and mash to smooth. Season with lemon juice, sugar, salt and pepper. Add butter and then taste and correct seasoning.

MUSHROOMS

Mushrooms make an excellent garnish, simply sautéed in butter and seasoned with salt and pepper. They are used in a variety of dishes, which include soups, sauces and fillings, and also served as appetizers.

Wild Mushrooms

There are hundreds of various wild mushrooms. Very few are actually poisonous, but most are inedible, either because of their taste or texture. Many types of wild mushrooms are very delicious (unfortunately including the poisonous ones). Unless you can positively identify what you are picking, it is best to purchase them from a reliable source. As a general rule, all poisonous mushrooms grow in the forest. Field mushrooms may make you sick but will not kill you. But don't depend on it, there are exceptions to every rule.

Some wild mushrooms are like a wet sponge (morels), releasing lot of juice in the pan. Others are quite dry (chanterelles, shitake). Accordingly, cooking them requires adjustments.

Dried mushrooms are very good in soups and as a flavoring in sauces. However, their texture, even after rehydration, remains leathery, making them unsuitable for side dishes.

Creamy Wild Mushrooms

Clean, wash and slice the mushrooms. Sauté them in butter over high heat until all juice evaporates. Add a little sherry or Madeira and reduce again. Add a little heavy cream and reduce to a thickened consistency. Season with salt and pepper. Garlic or shallots can be added while sautéing.

Note: all wild mushrooms are best consumed well-cooked. Some False Morels and Honey Caps contain small amounts of toxin, which is volatile and evaporates during cooking.

Grilled Mushrooms

Large, firm mushrooms such as cepes (porcini), shiitakes and portobellos, can be brushed with garlic butter or olive oil and grilled in the same way as a steak. Season them with salt and pepper.

Mushroom Strudel

Dice mushrooms and prepare according to the recipe for Creamy Mushrooms, but reduce them to very dry and dust with a little flour to bind well. Let them cool completely.

Roll out a sheet of puff dough or stack several sheets of phyllo dough (each brushed with butter). Place a row of mushrooms about 1 1/2 inch thick at the long edge of the dough and roll it up into a sausage shape to encase them. Brush the seam with beaten egg to seal, and brush the top also. Let rest in the refrigerator for one hour and then bake at 450° F. to brown. Slice on an angle, using a sharp bread knife, very gently. Excellent first course or garnish.

Stuffed Mushroom Caps with Ham Duxelles

Select some large button mushroom caps. Wash them, break the stems off and save. Sauté the caps over medium heat in a little clarified butter or vegetable oil until cooked.

Drain them well, return juice to cooking pan and reduce to dry. While the caps are cooking, dice the stems and about equal amounts of ham and onions.

Add the onions to the butter left from cooking the caps, cook until transparent, add the ham and the stems, and then cook until all juice evaporates. Dust with a little flour, add a splash of sherry and a little heavy cream and cook a while to thicken the mixture. Allow to cool.

Chop a ¼ cup of parsley and stir it into the cooled mixture. Using a spoon, mound the mixture into the cooked caps, topping each with a dollop of sour cream. Before serving, bake in 400° F. oven until heated through and lightly browned. Serve as first course or garnish.

Stuffed Morels with Wild Rice, Ham, Pecans & Scallions

(6 servings)

12 large or 18 medium-sized morels	1/3 cup pecans, quartered and toasted
1/2 cup heavy cream	1/4 cup scallions, finely sliced
1 whole egg	salt and pepper to taste
1 1/2 cup cooked wild rice	1/3 cup melted butter
1/3 cup smoked ham, chopped fine	

Preheat oven to 400° F. Wash the morels by briefly immersing them in tepid water. Do not soak them; agitate gently and then lift them out of the water. Cut the stems off and chop them (the stems). Look inside caps for any hiding insects or pine needles.

Mix cream and egg, and then add the rest of the ingredients, including chopped stems, except the butter. Stuff the morels with this mixture.

Butter a suitable non-aluminum pan (glass, ceramic, stainless steel) and line the morels in as one layer. Spoon the rest of the butter over them. Cover the pan and place in the oven. Bake for approximately 18 minutes, or until heated through, depending on size. If there is too much juice in the pan, place it on top of stove and cook down to a syrupy consistency.

To serve, divide morels between plates and spoon juice over. This dish can be served either as a garnish on a plate with wild game, or as a separate appetizer course.

SECTION: MARINADES

In the kitchen, game is marinated for three reasons: to tenderize, flavor and preserve. Basic marinades can be raw or cooked. Cooked marinades (brines) are used for longer marination of larger pieces. They are meant to be used only once and then discarded.

Raw marinades are for smaller pieces, kept for shorter times. The ingredients included in most raw marinades are commonly used later in sauce preparations, but caution must be exercised in using the liquid parts, so that the sauce does not get too acidic or salty.

RAW MARINADE #1

Use on venison, bison, rabbits or hares. Sufficient for 4-5 lbs of meat.

1 cup sliced carrots

1 cup sliced root celery or root parsley

1 cup sliced onions

3 Tbsp crushed black peppercorns

½ Tbsp crushed allspice berries

¼ Tbsp crushed juniper berries

4 bay leaves

2 Tbsp coriander

2 Tbsp thyme leaves

1 1/2 cup dry white wine

1/3 cup cider vinegar

Mix the ingredients together in a stainless steel, plastic, ceramic or glass bowl. Never marinate in aluminum! Place a layer of vegetables and spices on the bottom, then the meat, layering with more vegetable and spice mix. Pour rest over the top, cover and refrigerate. Turn over daily for two to seven days.

For larger pieces, you can use heavy plastic bags.

RAW MARINADE #2

Use with wild boar, bear or lamb. Sufficient for 5-6 lbs of meat.

1/4 cup crushed black peppercorns

1/2 cup lemon juice

2 Tbsp cup rosemary leaves

1 cup salad oil

4 Tbsp dry basil

1/4 cup chopped garlic

2 Tbsp thyme leaves

6 bay leaves

Mix together; rub over entire meat surface. When covered, can be refrigerated for as many as five days.

COOKED MARINADE

Using the same ingredients as in Raw Marinade #1, cook the vegetables in a small amount oil until tender without browning them, and then add the liquids. Replace wine with water, and the formula will be one part water and one part vinegar. Brink it to a boil, then allow to cool completely before adding meat. Marinate for up to 10 days.

RED WINE MARINADES

These are used in preparation of stews and braised meats, when meat discoloration due to the presence of tannin does not cause a problem. Hasenpfeffer (literally, "hare-pepper") falls into this category, but this preparation can be used on venison (Bourguignonne) and other game stews as well as on hare and rabbits. It can also be used to marinate pot roasts.

2 cups sliced onions	1 Tbsp each of thyme, rosemary
¼ cup crushed peppercorns	2 Tbsp chopped garlic
4 crushed juniper berries	1 bottle dry red wine
3 bay leaves	

Mix all together, add meat (whole or cut up), stir, cover and refrigerate for as many as four days. The meat is then well drained and separated from the vegetables, so it can be browned. All of the marinade and vegetables are used in the sauce preparation.

CHINESE MARINADE

Use with duck & goose breasts and pork.

1 cup light soy sauce	1 Tbsp sugar
1 Tbsp Szechuan peppercorns, crushed	1 1/2 Tbsp fresh ginger, grated
4 Tbsp peanut oil	2 Tbsp onion, finely chopped or mashed
1 Tbsp black peppercorns, crushed	3 cloves garlic, mashed
1/2 Tbsp chinese five-spice	

Combine all together, mix the meat in, place all in a non-reactive pan, cover and refrigerate overnight.

MARINADE FOR PHEASANTS OR GROUSE

1/3 cup brandy

1 cup medium-dry sherry

1/2 carrot, thinly sliced

1/2 celery branch, thinly sliced

1/2 small onion, thinly sliced

5 bay leaves

1 Tbsp thyme leaves

1/4 cup black peppercorns

This marinade will suffice for three to four birds. Dip the birds into the liquid, one at a time. Make sure the cavity gets treated. Mix the vegetables and spices in the remaining liquid. Place a layer of vegetables in a stainless plan, set the birds in and pour the rest over. Cover and refrigerate for as many as three days.

GAME SPICE

1 cup ground black pepper

1/4 cup ground thyme

1/8 cup ground allspice

1/8 cup ground bay leaves

1/4 cup ground juniper berries

1/4 cup ground coriander

Using a spice grinder, grinding your own herbs and spices will produce a superior quality blend. Mix together and keep in tightly-closed container. Use on all game birds, pates, roasts, etc.

CLARIFIED BUTTER

For sautéing or roasting, it is best to clarify your butter first. Whole butter contains a large quantity of milk which, when exposed to high temperatures, will burn before the butter fat does and leave black specks on your food.

To clarify butter, place a pound or more into a tall container. Set this container into a larger one, partially filled with hot water. Over low heat allow the butter to completely melt down. When melted, skim surface scum off. Using a small ladle, scoop the clear upper part of the butter into another container. This is your clarified butter. You can use the remaining milky residue to flavor or cook vegetables. Store clarified butter in closed containers, refrigerated.

Do not try to clarify the butter by melting it over the direct heat of a burner. Rather than separating, the butter will emulsify and become difficult to clarify unless you continue to cook it to the point when it browns and all the liquid evaporates. This is then called "brown butter".

CAESAR SALAD

Dressing:

2 whole eggs

1/3 cup fresh squeezed lemon juice

2 tsp salt

1 tsp sugar

2 tsp fresh coarse ground pepper

1/2 tsp Worcestershire sauce

2 1/2 cups olive oil

1 rounded Tbsp mashed garlic

1 rounded Tbsp mashed anchovy fillets

1/2 cup coffee cream

Very important! For proper emulsification, place all ingredients at room temperature. Place eggs, lemon juice, salt, sugar, pepper and Worcestershire sauce in a blender. Turn the blender on and start adding oil in a thin trickle; after the first cup of oil is absorbed, you can increase the flow of oil, providing the emulsification proceeds properly. After all the oil is added, whip in the garlic, anchovies and cream.

Refrigerate for future use; this dressing will keep for three weeks if properly handled.

For a salad: Prepare croutons cut from white bread, sprinkled with butter and baked in a medium oven until golden brown. Grate good quality Parmesan cheese. Cut romaine lettuce into 1½ inch strips, wash and dry. Toss the romaine with dressing, then add the grated cheese and croutons.

INDIAN SALAD

(6 servings)

While this is not an authentic Indian recipe, try to buy imported Madras curry powder. Locally made curries are not as good.

Dressing:

1/4 cup salad oil

2 Tbsp Madras curry powder

1 clove garlic, mashed

1 tsp salt

2 Tbsp lemon juice

1 Tbsp Dijon mustard

1/4 cup olive oil

In a small sauce pan, heat the salad oil with curry until it starts to sizzle. Immediately add the garlic and rest of the ingredients. Using a whip, mix all together.

For the salad, you will need:

2 heads chicory	1 red onion, sliced into rings
2 oranges, sectioned	1/4 cup shredded coconut

Toss the ingredients with a little dressing, taste and add more if needed. Serve with roasts.

CELERIAC SALAD

Celeriac is also known as knob or root celery. The top part is not edible, except for the very young leaves, which can be used as an herb.

Equipment: stiff brush, peeler, knife, stainless pot, bowl, whisk & spoon.

Scrub the celeriac using a stiff brush under running water, then peel it and remove all the fine roots. Use the trimmings in stocks and marinades.

Cut the celeriac into quarters and put it in a stainless pot. Cover with water. Add a little salt and bring to a simmer. After about 10 minutes, when tender but firm, drain it and let cool. Slice it into thin slices. Place these in a bowl and add some thin-sliced onion. Season with a simple vinaigrette as follows:

1/2 cup olive oil	1 Tbsp sugar
1/3 cup white wine vinegar (see below)	3 Tbsp Dijon mustard
salt	1 tsp fresh ground pepper

Using a whisk, mix all ingredients together. Add the vinaigrette to the celeriac a little at a time, tasting as you add, until pleasing acidity is achieved.

Note: Celeriac cooks faster than potatoes. Do not overcook it! As in other dishes, the ultimate taste depends on the quality of the ingredients, especially the oil and vinegar used. Varies types of vinegar, such as cider or tarragon, can be used. Malt and balsamic vinegars, while tasty, will give the salad a slightly brownish tint.

This salad is very popular in Germany and Austria. It goes very well with many wild game dishes, particularly venison. Made in advance, it will keep in a refrigerator for up to two weeks.

GINGER SAUCE

1 cup red currant jelly or orange marmalade

1/2 cup Major Grey (mango) chutney

1/4 cup lemon juice

1/4 cup medium-dry sherry

1 Tbsp grated fresh ginger root

1 tsp powdered (dry) ginger

zest of ½ orange, grated

zest of ½ lemon, grated

Place all ingredients in a blender or processor and blend until smooth. Refrigerated, this sauce will keep for a month or more. Goes well with grilled birds and pates.

APPLE HORSERADISH RELISH

2 large tart apples

1/2 cup prepared horseradish

lemon juice or sugar to taste

Peel the apples and grate them finely into a bowl. Mix with horseradish; keep refrigerated. Serve with domestic or wild pork dishes, also boiled beef.

CRANBERRY-ORANGE RELISH

Try this refreshing recipe in place of a traditional cranberry sauce! Very good accompaniment with game of various types, also roast or sautéed veal and poultry dishes.

12 oz package fresh or frozen cranberries

1 medium orange, quartered and seeded, peel left on

3/4 cup granulated sugar

2 Tbsp cherry brandy (Kirsch, optional)

Wash the cranberries (if fresh). Place them in a food processor, along with all other ingredients, and chop to kernel size. Keep the relish refrigerated until use.

THE FINAL WORD

For many people, cooking wild game is a scary proposition. It need not be that way.

These recipes and ideas should help you produce dishes you would be proud of serving to your most important guests. Their aim is to enable you to handle your next wild harvest with confidence.

As always, the quality of your ingredients will impact the final dish. Using short cuts, such as canned mushrooms or vegetables, will only produce mediocre results. Additionally, remember that good wild game cooking does not start in the kitchen. Great wild game preparations begin in the field immediately after the hunters bag their game, with proper handling, care, cooling and aging. You cannot accomplish outstanding meals with game that was poorly handled and prepared. I trust that my advice will provide you with a special kind of "guide service," leading to more confident cooking and enjoyable eating for you and your family.

Good hunting, fishing and good cooking!

-- Chef Milos

PART 2:

FISH AND SEAFOOD

HANDLING FISH

How we handle the fish we catch immediately after we get them out of the water will make a difference later. Keeping them alive is the best way. Another way is to place them in a cooler with ice. Once they expire, it is very important to hold them as close to 32° F. as possible.

Removing the entrails and gills will lengthen the holding time. Whole or gutted fish can be buried in ice, leaving drainage open. Wash fillets briefly in cold water, but avoid soaking them. Clean fillets should then be packed in plastic bags and not come in direct contact with ice or water any more. To freeze your catch, the most important thing is to keep the air out of the container. To thaw the fish later, place it in your refrigerator. Never re-freeze thawed fish.

PURCHASING FISH

Some of us may prefer to *catch the fish* in a store, unaware of the process that goes on in the fishing industry. The quality of wild fresh water fish is related to the proximity of source.

Regarding Atlantic Ocean fish, we have to realize the situation the fishermen are facing. Back in the fifties, *day boats* left the harbor in the evening, fished all night and returned to harbor in the morning. That was really fresh fish! Due to depletion of fish stocks and shore pollution, day boat fishing is not economically feasible any more. Today, larger fishing boats have to go 60 miles out to sea to start fishing. That takes a lot of fuel and, depending on their success, the boats may stay there up to 3 weeks. The boats take a huge load of crushed ice with them. The fish they catch is gutted and placed in large, flat wooden boxes and ice is shoveled over them. When the box is full, another box is stacked on top and so on. The sheer weight of fish and ice, plus the time the boat stays on the water take their toll. As the boat is returning to harbor, the captain radios his expected docking time to a buyer from a seafood company that specializes in high quality fish such as Foley's in Boston. The buyer will be at the dock ready. The fish caught the last two days is called *the top of the catch*. It gets unloaded first and commands as much as three times the price of the fish on the bottom. As the conveyor belt brings the fish from the boat to the dock, the buyer picks out the best looking, freshest fish. He pays the captain cash on the spot. The content of the next few boxes is purchased by fish distributors that service upscale restaurants and stores. The rest of the haul is then sold sight unseen at auction to supermarket buyers. The *top of the catch* fish is rushed to the plant where it is immediately processed in refrigerated rooms. Then it is packed in either plastic or metal trays, which are stacked in insulated cardboard boxes, labeled and promptly taken to the airport. Customers all over the country, willing to pay the price, get fish which has been at the most 3-4 days out of the water. That kind of freshness does not come cheap!

I will explain the methods serious chefs use in buying fish:

To start, they deal with reputable companies which guarantee the authenticity and freshness of their products. Then they personally inspect the shipment on arrival. Many tricks are involved in making old fish look and smell fresh, such as *dipping* and *gassing*. An expert can tell.

The average supermarket does not sell really fresh sea fish, no matter where they are located. They just cannot afford the price. Some unscrupulous merchants sell previously frozen and then thawed fish as fresh. Such fish have watery, spongy, opaque flesh. Whole fresh fish have bulging eyes, bright red gills, bright colored scales or skin, unbroken fins and tails and smell like sea or cucumbers, rather than "fishy". Looking inside a whole fish, the ribs should be firmly attached, not protruding out. The specks of blood by the spine are red, not brown. If you smell any hint of yeast or ammonia, reject the fish. Fish fillets appear translucent and are shiny twice: once when very fresh, second time when they are putrid. Dull, opaque fillets are not fresh. If you want a specific type of fish (snapper, grouper, cod), do not buy skinless fillets, which could be anything but the genuine article.

We have no true sole around our coasts. Any native fish called sole is in fact some type of flounder, and there are several. The only real sole available is the Dover sole, imported from England. Genuine Florida red snapper is seldom seen in stores. Most likely it is a South American cousin. Red fish is probably black fish, Norwegian salmon could be Chilean and Cape scallops could be bays, which are much inferior. Fresh scallops look glossy and there is no juice in the container. If they look opaque white and there is juice, they have been soaked in chemical solutions (ascorbic acid, tri-sodium phosphate) to increase their weight and destroy odor.

Shrimp from the Gulf of Mexico come graded by size and color. White are best, pink a close second, brown are less expensive (shell color is determined by the amount of iodine in them). All shrimp in stores are or have been frozen. Imported tiger shrimp from the Far East are raised in "fresh" water ponds, often polluted with sewage. Large shrimp are sometimes called *prawns*. *Langoustines* are a species of small lobster from the North Sea.

Clam juice comes from several sources, some slightly better than dirty fish water. Read labels.

Much imported fish is turned away at the border by health authorities because of unsanitary conditions and high bacterial count.

BASIC FISH COOKING METHODS

Overcooking is probably the most common mistake cooks make when preparing fish.

Most fish do not take long to cook, so they are prepared "to order". They should not be cooked in advance and reheated. This is not that difficult to accomplish. Sauces and garnishes can be prepared well in advance; the rest of the ingredients you will need can be assembled. With everything at hand, all you need to do is cook the fish and start serving.

Lean fish are more prone to overcooking, as they will dry out faster and become crumbly. The health authorities and some cookbooks advocate cooking fish to 145° F. internal temperature. Undoubtedly, this is the safest way to destroy any bacteria and parasites. We also need to consider, that after being removed from the heat source, the internal temperature of fish, as well as meats, continues to rise. It is called *carry-over cooking*. If you cook a large piece of fish to 145 F internal temperature, after you allow it to sit for 10 minutes, it will be 160 F and dried out. While eating sushi does present the danger of ingesting parasites, most bacteria present on a fish would be on the surface, which gets more heat exposure than the inside. Sturgeon, eel, catfish and monkfish are better when cooked well done. Tuna needs to be consumed raw or at least very rare.

The most common fish cooking method in this country is fried. Some people do not like to cook fish in their homes because of the odor they leave. There are several ways to cook fish leaving almost no smell and still achieving great taste. Examples are *steaming* and *poaching*, which also retains their natural flavor and is healthier for us. Another is *Grilling* on an outdoor barbecue, which gives great taste. Preparing the fish you caught for cooking is another subject. Some people may need help with it. It is not a very difficult job!

FILLETING PAN FISH

1. Make an incision under the pectoralfin to the spine

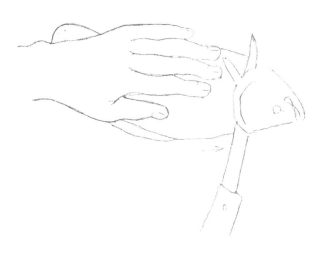

2. Holding the Knife in a horizontal position starting at the head and following just above the bones, make an incision through the center of the back. The point of the knife should be sliding along the spine.

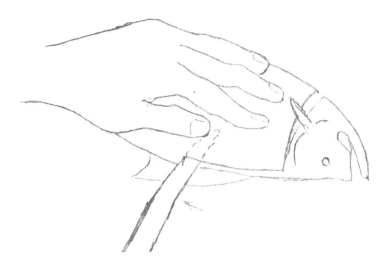

3. As your knife reaches opposite of vent, push the knife through and cut the rest of the upper fillet towards the tail.

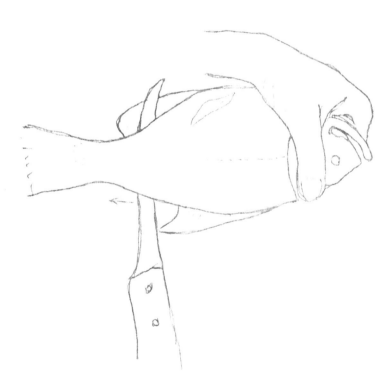

4. Holding the partially detached upper fillet with your spare hand, lift the point of the knife slightly to slide over the rib cage, completing the filleting. Repeat on opposite side.

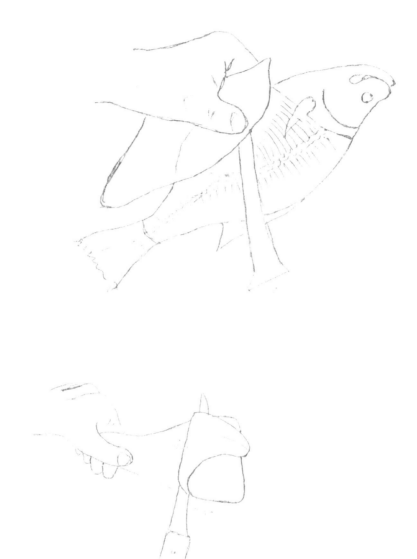

5. Skin the Fillet as in above direction.

FISH AND SEAFOOD VIDEOS

To view a preparation and cooking of fish and seafood, Jerry Chiappetta and myself have produced tapes, called "Wild Harvest Videos" now available on DVDs at Amazon.

COOKING DEFINITIONS

Poaching: Cooking fish submerged in liquid called "court bouillon" at temperatures between 165° F. and 180° F. We may poach whole fish, fillets or individual portions. Poaching will take longer to cook, but produces a moist fish, very pleasant to eat. Boiling will result in a dry, crumbly fish. Poached fish could be served warm or cold.

Steaming: Cooking individual portions or whole small fish either in a perforated pan or a Chinese steamer tightly covered and placed over boiling water, to which aromatic herbs, spices and vegetables are added.

Oven steaming: In a buttered, casserole-type dish, with some liquid added, covered.

Sautéing: Same as pan-frying, but with less fat.

Grilling or barbecuing: Grilling directly on the grate or in a wire basket or in a foil pouch. Whether we have a charcoal, electric, gas, or wood-fired grill or barbecue, the methods are similar. Without any equipment, we may grill small fish on a stick held over a campfire.

Smoking: Could be done either with cold smoke or hot smoke, depending on the results we want. We may also pan-smoke or barbecue grill-smoke.

Roasting: Certain firm-fleshed fish could be roasted either whole or in fillets.

Baking: We may bake small or larger fish or portions, stuffed or plain, sometimes wrapped in sheets of dough, parchment or foil.

En papillote: Small fish or portions, parchment wrapped, then baked in an oven.

Deep frying: This least healthy method is still enjoyed by many folks. There are numerous batters and coatings employed. The type of fat we use to fry the fish will make a great difference in the taste. While clarified butter gives the best taste, it burns easily and has a short life. Peanut oil is probably the best all-around and could be blended with some clarified butter. People allergic to peanuts can use safflower, soy or canola oil.

Blackening: Cajun style is brushing the fish with oil or butter, then coating it with a blend of herbs and spices and searing it in a very hot, dry cast iron skillet to blacken both sides of the fish. Open the windows; lots of smoke develops!

Fish soups: We can make great tasting soups with many kinds of fish and seafood, clear or creamy. In order to keep the fish and seafood moist, they should NEVER boil. For clear soups, we cook the broth first, then cook the vegetables in it and *poach* the fish in the finished soup just before serving. When cooking French Bouillabaisse or Italian Cioppino, we add the seafood components to the broth gradually, according to the length of time they take to cook.

With thickened and cream-type soups, we poach the fish in stock and lift it out to be picked for bones and added later. We use the resulting broth to make the soup, adding the cooked fish before serving. You may reheat a fish soup, but avoid boiling it with the fish.

Fish "Boils": Traditionally made with potatoes and corn, on the shores of a Minnesota lake. Anytime we combine various ingredients, we have to consider how long it will take to cook each one. We cannot throw the fish in the pot with the potatoes. By the time the potatoes are cooked, the fish will turn to a mush! So we would put the potatoes in the pot first and barely cover them with water. Then we would add seasoning, bring it to a boil and about 15 minutes later, add any root vegetables if desired. When the potatoes are just about done we add the fish and 2 minutes later the corn. At that point we would turn the heat off and let the fish slowly cook in the broth to done. We must NEVER boil the fish!

THE RUINED TROUT

It is hard to beat very fresh fish, simply sautéed in butter or olive oil. I recall an elk hunting trip in the Colorado Rockies many years ago. We spent a week in miserable rainy weather, sleeping in tents, surviving on dehydrated food rations. After filling my tag we returned to the ranch and I still had a few days left before the plane departure.

There was a trout stream running through the ranch and I set out to catch a dinner. Upon my return I cleaned the cutthroat trout and offered to cook them, but the rancher's wife adamantly refused my offer, without any explanation. I guessed she did not trust my cooking.

I was drooling thinking about the succulent dinner we were going to have. When it arrived at the table, my jaw dropped. The beautiful trout were coated with corn meal and fried in shortening to a point where you could lift them up by the tail like bread sticks. I almost cried!

SAUTÉING FISH

Most any fish can be sautéed. The size of the pan should always accommodate the fish without crowding. Use two skillets if necessary. Small fish are cooked whole. The cooking temperature depends on the thickness of the fish. Thin fillets are sautéed over high heat, thicker fish over medium heat. Regardless which method you use to cook it, the fish should never be turned over more than once, as it may break.

Season the fish with salt just before cooking and dust with flour.

When placing filleted fish in a pan, or on a grill, we always place it first skin side up (even if it is skinned), turn it over at half time and finish it skin side down. We plate it as it comes out of the pan or off the grill, without turning it again.

To speed up cooking of a thick whole fish, you may *score* it by making crossways incisions into it about one inch apart. When sautéing thicker cuts of fish, you may put a lid on the pan after you turn the fish and then lower the heat, or place the uncovered pan in a 350° F. oven to finish cooking it.

For health reasons, you may sauté the fish without flouring it, in a stick-free pan, with only a few drops of oil.

All fish will stay moister when cooked with the skin on. The skin of cod and haddock is not only edible, but delicious and very nutritional. However, the skin of some fish imparts a very strong, unpleasant taste and should be removed before cooking. This is especially true of (fresh water) smallmouth and largemouth bass.

We remove the scales of fish to be cooked with the skin on, except those with very fine scales, such as speckled trout. We peel the skin off catfish and eel, using pliers. Underneath the skin there is a brownish or reddish layer of flesh, which is the lateral line, sometimes referred to as the "mud vein" or "blood vein." On some oily fish it is very strong tasting and if the fish comes from polluted waters, it contains much of the contaminants. To remove the lateral line, either slightly raise the edge of the knife while skinning the fish, or after the skinning, trim the darker part off using a very sharp, thin bladed knife.

To check the doneness of a fish fillet, slide a large spatula half way under it, then lift the point of the spatula up. As the center of the fillet lifts up, it will crack open revealing the inside. If there is any translucency, it needs a little more cooking. Solid opaque color indicates the fish is done. As you lower the point of the spatula back down, the crack will close up again and conceal the fact that you have "peeked" inside someone's fish!

To check the doneness of a steak-cut fish, such as salmon, insert a kitchen fork into the spine. If the spine comes out easily, the fish is done. You can then peel the skin off by rolling it up on a table fork, like opening a can of sardines. Some fish, such as the Atlantic salmon, are better when slightly undercooked. Other fish, such as sturgeon, eel, catfish and monkfish are better slightly overcooked.

Small fish, such as perch, bluegills, speckled trout and small ocean fish are best cooked whole, only gutted and gills removed. They retain more moisture. Small trout are cooked and served with the head on. To check doneness of whole fish, look inside at the spine, which should be gray and show no pinkness or transparency.

BROILING FISH

We broil whole small fish or cuts of larger ones. The technique is the same.

Again, to keep fish moist, it is best to cook it with the skin on. You may sprinkle a light dusting of paprika on the skinless side for color, season it with salt and pepper, brush it with oil or butter, sprinkle with a little bread crumbs. We place the fish on the broiling plate skin side down, and if necessary, finish it in a hot oven. The skin will stick to the pan and if desired, using a wide spatula, we may lift the clean fillet off, leaving the skin behind.

We do NOT turn thin fish fillets when broiling them as they would break apart.

The taste of broiled fish will improve by marinating it for an hour before cooking with a little lemon juice or dry vermouth and oil.

Broiling, steaming and poaching are the healthiest methods of cooking fish. If you want to totally eliminate the cooking fat, you need not put any on the fish. However, broiled fish will look and taste better with just a little brushing of butter, oil or some dressing.

A half inch thick fillet will take about 4 minutes, thicker ones longer. Cook to firm only - overcooking will cause dryness. To check doneness, see sautéing fish. Serve broiled fish with lemon wedges and a sauce on the side (see recipes).

GRILLING (SOME CALL IT BARBECUING) FISH BASICS

Almost any fish can be grilled in a similar way we grill meat or poultry, except that greater care must be taken in handling it so it does not fall apart.

Depending on the size and firmness of the fish, it can be either placed directly on the grill or grilled in a wire basket. There are two types of grilling baskets: a flat one for small fish and fillets and a "torpedo"-shaped one for larger pieces or whole fish.

They both have hinged tops and make fish grilling very easy.

Without these baskets, you may also grill fish in a pouch made of heavy aluminum foil. Whether you use a gas, electric, charcoal or wood grill, the procedure is the same.

When placing the fish directly on the grill, the grate should be very clean and oiled to prevent sticking. Leaving the skin on will keep the fish moister and easier to handle.

You may marinate the fish a couple of hours before cooking with a little lemon juice and vegetable oil. You may also baste it during grilling with a little melted butter.

The intensity of the heat should be proportionate to the thickness of the fish: thin pieces are cooked over higher heat, thicker ones over lower heat to give them time to cook through.

A wood-fired grill gives the best taste, imparting a light smoky flavor to the fish. Hardwood chips, soaked in advance in water and added to the hot coals, also work well. Softwood should be avoided, as it contains creosote and tar, which produce bitter smoke and is carcinogenic. Where hardwood is not available we may use softwood, providing that we build a huge fire and let it burn down to glowing, smokeless embers, before grilling. Some fish, such as salmon, are best cooked a little underdone to keep them from drying out.

TO GRILL FISH

To prevent sticking, pat the surface of the fish dry with paper towels before cooking. Season it with salt and pepper and you may also add some herbs, such as tarragon, thyme, dill or basil. Then brush it with vegetable oil or clarified butter (see sautéed walleye) on both sides, then sprinkle it lightly or dip it in bread crumbs, which will prevent sticking.

COOKING DIRECTLY ON THE GRILL

Use a medium-hot grill. If you have a type of grill with a hinged lid, place the fish skin-side down on it and close the lid. The fish need not be turned and will cook through. The skin will stick to the grill. Using a wide spatula you may scoop the cooked fish up, leaving the skin behind.

If you do not have a lid over the grill, or if you would like to have the grill marks visible on the fish, then place it skin-side up on the grid. Depending on the type of fish (pike, walleye), you may be better off skinning it first. After approximately two minutes, you may reposition the fish by turning it 90 degrees sideways to get the "X" markings on. When the fish is half-cooked, turn it over, skin-side down. Depending on the thickness of the fish, you may now put the lid on, or invert a pan over the fish to trap some hot air under it and speed up the cooking.

Fillets of walleye, pike, whitefish and catfish can be grilled over a fairly hot fire and will be done after turning over. I have Canadian friends who did not believe a northern pike is good to eat until I grilled it for them over charcoal fire.

TO GRILL IN A FLAT, HINGED BASKET

Line up the seasoned, buttered and crumb-coated fish in the basket in one layer. You may overlap thin fillets. Small perch, bluegills, brook trout and small ocean fish should be left whole, just gutted and washed. They will yield much more meat that way. There is no need to scale them: you can easily peel the skin off and lift the fillets out after cooking. The bones will remain attached to the spine!

Close the basket and over a fairly hot fire brown fish on one side, turn basket over and brown on the other side. To check for doneness, look inside the fish at the spine. When grey, the fish are done. When pink, cook a little longer. You will be amazed how moist and flavorful they come out.

TO GRILL IN ALUMINUM FOIL

In camp grounds and tourist areas the grills usually have very wide grates, making it difficult to grill fish. Without bringing your own equipment, you can solve the problem using foil. Cut a piece of heavy duty foil twice the length of the grill. Cut another one and place on top of the first one to make a double layer. If your foil is flimsy, make four layers.

With the point of a knife, poke holes in it about three inches apart, all over, to allow steam to escape. Season and line up the prepared fish over half of the foil in a single layer, then fold the other half of the foil over and crimp the edges to seal. Place thus formed pouch on a hot grill, cook about 5 minutes on one side, flip it over and finish on the other side.

To check for doneness, carefully open one side of the foil pouch to take a look inside the fish. If not done, re-close it and grill a little longer.

Most campgrounds do not provide any firewood. Hardwood could be hard to find. You may use softwood, but you need to burn a lot of it to produce enough glowing timbers to cook over. Do not grill on a live softwood fire. It will have a creosote taste.

BAKING FISH

We may bake whole medium-to-larger sized fish in a roasting pan or smaller fish on sizzling platters or sheet pans. We leave the head and skin (scaled) on the fish for baking. Medium to large whole fish will need 325° F. oven temperatures and frequent basting. If we stuff the fish, it is best to bone it out completely first. That way we do not have to worry about the bones getting mixed with the stuffing. Bake the fish to 145° F. internal temp. After removing it from the oven, allow it to rest a while before carving.

To debone a whole fish (head left on) for baking or poaching, without breaking it apart:

1. Lay the fish on its side. Starting near the head, push a knife horizontally through the rib cage just above the spine, but do not cut completely through the back side.

2. Slide the knife along the spine towards the tail. Stop about an inch before the tail.

3. Turn the fish over and repeat on the other side.

The spine should now be loosened from the flesh on both sides. Sever the spine at the head and tail and remove it.

4. Lay the fish on its back and open it up. Slide a sharp, thin-bladed knife under the rib cage on one side and remove the bones. Repeat on the other side.

5. Slide a knife along both sides of the dorsal fin and pull it out. Cut off the pelvic fins.

6. On a larger fish, such as salmon, pull out the pin bones using needle-nose pliers.

You are now ready to stuff the fish. To keep the stuffing in a larger fish, you may sew the opening closed. With a smaller fish you need not bother. To prevent larger fish from sticking to the roasting pan, place it on a greased parchment paper.

FISH STUFFINGS

Avoid the temptation to use turkey-type stuffing. It will not taste good. Fish stuffing should be mild, so it does not compete with the fish flavor. For smaller fish, simply sautéed, sliced mushrooms, seasoned and lightly dusted with flour to hold them together, are very good. For larger fish, you may consider crabmeat, bound together with a small amount of fish "forcemeat". To make that, place about 1 cup of raw, boneless fish in a processor, add ½ cup heavy cream, salt and cayenne pepper, and puree it to a smooth consistency. Transfer it to a mixing bowl, fold the crabmeat into it, add some chopped parsley for color and stuff the fish.

STIR-FRYING FISH

A non-stick wok or skillet works best when stir-frying fish. Use only firm-fleshed fish such as catfish, sturgeon, Dover sole, or crustaceans as shrimp, scallops or lobster. Softer fish will fall apart.

If you want to serve it over rice, start cooking the rice first, then 15 minutes later start stir-frying. Have all ingredients ready at hand, vegetables and seafood cut, pans, seasonings ready. For vegetables, use scallions, bean sprouts, sugar snap peas, asparagus, zucchini, mushrooms, red peppers, etc. Avoid green peppers, as they are too dominant. Cut the larger vegetables into neat, bite-sized pieces, not too small.

Combinations of several fish are very nice. Use small amount of peanut or safflower oil. Stir-fry them in batches not larger than to cover the bottom of your pan in one layer. Do not stir the fish too much or it will break up and you may wind up with fish hash. Do not use salt if you are using soy sauce. Pepper is O.K.

It is best to turn the fish only once. The pan must be clean and hot before you add more oil and fish. The fish should not be wet and you need not flour it, although it will help prevent sticking if you do. Do not overcook, remove them when half done. They will be just right when you are done cooking. Remove the fish to another dish, put the vegetables in the pan and if needed, add a little more oil.

Stir-fry the vegetables until they turn a vibrant color, then return the fish to them. Season the dish with a splash of soy sauce and a little cayenne pepper. If you wish, you may add a tablespoon of corn starch dissolved in 3 Tbsp of sherry wine to thicken it a little. Make circles of rice on plates, spoon the stir-fry into the center. Serve immediately, do not hold and reheat.

The quality and freshness of all ingredients will be directly reflected in the finished dish. Using canned vegetables or mushrooms will produce very mediocre results, not worth doing.

THE FRIED FISH DISASTER

During the war, food was scarce. Cooking fats were especially hard to obtain. When my mother was in the hospital, my dad's sister volunteered to cook dinner for us. One day I came home from work and noticed a strange, petroleum-like odor in the kitchen. "What smells?" I asked. That was the wrong thing to say to my aunt, who was very touchy about any remarks. I got scolded immediately. As we apprehensively sat down, afraid to make any more comments, she served us fried fish. Taking the first bite, the fish immediately congealed on our teeth and the roof of our mouths. We looked at each other, wondering what happened.

"What kind of fat did you use for frying, auntie?" I meekly asked. "Well, the suet I found in the pantry!" she replied angrily.

My brother studied chemistry and brought home a slab of paraffin wax for his experiments. She mistook it for suet. After explaining to her what happened, she lectured us about not keeping things in their proper place. Probably feeling her reputation as a great cook was now irreparably tarnished, she then took off in a huff. It was comical, except that we had to find an alternate dinner.

FRYING FISH

Although this cooking method is the least healthy, many people still love fried fish. There are several methods of coating the fish prior to cooking. These are:

Three-Step Breading:

This is the most basic one in which you coat the seasoned pieces with flour, egg wash and bread or cracker crumbs.

I do not like **store-bought bread crumbs**, which contain chemical preservatives. You can make your own two types: fresh or dried. Both are easy to make. For **fresh bread crumbs** use soft white sandwich bread, crust trimmed off. Place the slices in a food processor and grind them into crumbs. For **dry bread crumbs**, use any white bread or rolls, completely dried out. Break it into pieces and grind it up in the food processor. Never store bread crumbs in a tightly-covered container (unless you freeze them), as they will get rancid.

TEMPURA BATTER

Tempura leaves the thinnest, crunchiest crust, which will turn soggy if not served immediately.

1 1/2 cups flour	1/8 tsp baking powder
1/2 cup corn starch	2 cups cold water
1/8 tsp baking soda	1 cup vegetable oil
2 Tbsp salt	1 egg
2 tsp sugar	

Stir the first 8 ingredients to a smooth batter. Stir in the egg last. Use peanut or safflower oil heated to 375° F. Dip skinless, thin fish fillets such as perch, bluegill or flounder in flour, shake off and dip in the batter. Drop them floating in the oil and fry to golden brown. Serve immediately, or the batter will turn soggy.

Serve with mashed potatoes and a Wasabi sauce on the side.

(Wasabi is a very pungent Japanese root similar to, but not related to horseradish.)

WASABI SAUCE

hot water

2 Tbsp dry wasabi powder (sold in stores)

1 tsp soy sauce

6 Tbsp mayonnaise

pinch of sugar

Stir a little hot water into the wasabi powder to make a smooth paste. Cover and let sit 10 min. Then stir in the rest of the ingredients. Thin with more water to sauce consistency.

A SIMPLE COATING

A simple coating is dipping the fish in milk, then dredging it in seasoned flour

(1 cup flour, 2 Tbsp paprika, 1 tsp salt, 1/4 tsp pepper sifted together).

Brook trout, perch or smelt are mostly coated this way (also fried zucchini and eggplant), which leaves only a thin crust. There are also commercially-produced breadings on the market.

BEER BATTER

1 1/4 cup flour

1 tsp salt

1/2 tsp paprika

1 Tbsp vegetable oil

1 egg

1 cup beer

Mix all ingredients to a smooth paste. Dip fish pieces in and deep fry in 360° F. oil. Pieces ½ inch thick will take approximately three to four minutes to cook. The most important part of frying is the quality of the fat, which will ultimately play a major role in the taste of the fried product. Shortening or margarine are the least desirable.

To reuse frying fat, strain it through a fine mesh strainer every time after use and discard sediment on the bottom. This, and refrigeration, will prolong its life. Once any fat starts foaming (not just a few bubbles, but all the fat turning to foam), it will no longer brown the items you are frying and you may as well throw it out.

Plain melted butter is unsuitable for frying or fast sautéing, as the whey in it will soon burn and produce black specks on the food. The best fat for frying is peanut or safflower oil, which has a high smoking point (tolerates high temperatures), is very mild tasting and lasts longer.

To make fried food less greasy, place it on a paper towel-covered sheet pan in a 350° F. oven for 3-4 minutes before serving it.

For garnishes, mashed potatoes go very well with fried items, together with a nice

simple salad, either green, or tomato, cucumber, etc. (see recipes).

You should avoid greasy garnishes, such as fried potatoes (fish and chips are a bad idea) or richly buttered vegetables. Simple lemon wedges are fine with fried fish, but a nice sauce, such as Tartar or Remoulade will further enhance your enjoyment.

SECTION: FRESHWATER FISH

FISH EYES??? SERIOUSLY?

At home, we occasionally had small, farm-raised rainbow trout for dinner. My wife always sautéed and served them with their heads on. One time, I showed my son who was about five years old how to pluck out and eat the cheek muscles. He asked me if he could also eat the eyes. Boys at that age lack inhibitions they may adopt later.

I remembered seeing a picture in a classical French cookbook of a "Finnish Eye Stew". It was a bowl of marble-sized eyeballs in sauce. Evidently the Finns make such a dish. So, to answer my son's question, I said "you can, if you want to". He promptly poked an eye of the trout out and put it in his mouth. Then he declared "Dad, it is really good! You should try it!" So, I figured if he can do it, so can I. I was amazed how rich the eye tasted. It had a slightly crunchy shell on the outside, with a jellied center. The pupil turned rubbery though.

Several weeks later my son was playing in the yard with Danny, a friend of his. It was getting close to meal time and my wife did not want to send the boy home, so she asked him if he would like to stay for lunch. He agreed to stay. My wife said: "We are having fish – do you eat fish?" He replied yes.

We all took our places around the table and my wife served each of us a plate with a trout and potatoes. Danny sat stiffly erect, his eyes wide open, staring at his plate, not touching anything. Unintentionally, to make the situation worse, my son said "Danny, you have to try the eyes, they taste great!" upon which he plucked an eye out of his trout and put it in his mouth. At that point Danny blurted "I am not hungry today" and blasted out of his chair. I was concerned he would break the door in his hurry to get out! My wife and I laughed so hard, we nearly fell out of our chairs. My son looked puzzled and inquired "What happened? Why did he leave?"

We assumed that the only fish Danny ever ate were Fish Sticks from the supermarket. We did not see Danny for three weeks after that. He probably told his mother we were cannibals!

WALLEYE SAUTÉED IN HAZELNUT CRUST

6 servings

3/4 cup fresh bread crumbs

1/2 cup clarified butter

3/4 cup finely ground hazelnuts

salt, pepper, flour

1 egg beaten w/ 2 Tbsp milk

6 walleye fillets, deboned and skinned, 6-8 oz each

To make fresh bread crumbs, trim the crust off fresh white bread, place the white part in a processor or mixer and grind up.

To make clarified butter, place butter in a tall pot set in a hot water bath over moderate heat. When completely melted, skim the foam off, then scoop out the clear butter, leaving the milky residue back.

Preheat oven to 350° F.; Preheat 2 large skillets to medium hot.

Mix hazelnuts with the bread crumbs. Season fish and dust with flour. Dip it in the beaten egg, then coat with hazelnut and crumb mixture on both sides. Shake excess crumbs off.

Heat butter in pans, place fish in. Brown nicely on one side; turn and brown the other side. Transfer fish to a cookie sheet, then place in the oven for about 5 minutes.

You may serve it simply with lemon wedges, or with a sauce (see recipes).

You may substitute hazelnuts with almonds, pecans or walnuts.

BLACKENED SMALLMOUTH BASS WITH PECAN BUTTER

6 servings

Mix together the following dried herbs and spices:

6 bass fillets, boneless and skinless, about 7 oz each

salt to taste

3 Tbsp vegetable oil

1/2 tsp cayenne

2 Tbsp paprika

1 Tbsp thyme

2 tsp ground cumin

1 Tbsp dry mustard

1 Tbsp tarragon

Preheat oven to 325° F.; Preheat two heavy, preferably cast iron skillets to smoking hot.

Season fish with salt, coat with oil on both sides and then roll in spice mixture. Place the fillets in the hot, dry skillets and pan- grill to dark brown on both sides.

Remove, place in 325° F. oven for 5 minutes to finish cooking.

Pecan butter:

1/2 cup butter	3/4 cup chopped pecans
3 Tbsp lemon juice	2 Tbsp chopped parsley

In a smaller pan brown the pecans in butter. Add lemon juice and parsley and spoon over fish.

Note 1: Different nuts may be used.

Note 2: You may also cook the fish on a hot grill.

GRILLED COHO SALMON WITH GINGER GLAZE

6 servings

6 salmon steaks, 8-10 oz each or fillets 6-8 oz each

Glaze:

1 cup clam juice	4 tsp lemon juice
1/2 tsp orange zest, grated	2 tsp mashed garlic
1/3 cup light soy sauce	1 anchovy fillet, mashed
1 Tbsp fresh ginger, grated	1 1/3 tsp corn starch
2 Tbsp orange marmalade	2 Tbsp med. sherry
1/4 tsp cayenne pepper	1/2 cup softened butter
4 tsp molasses	

Glaze:

In a saucepan reduce clam juice by boiling to 1/2 cup. Add next 9 ingredients and bring back to a simmer. Mix corn starch with sherry, stir into sauce to thicken. Remove from fire, whip in softened butter.

For Grilling:

1/4 cup melted butter or oil   bread crumbs

Preheat the grill to medium hot. Brush fish with butter or oil on both sides and sprinkle lightly with bread crumbs. Grill the steaks: depending on their thickness about 5 minutes on one side, turn over and finish cooking on the other side. Should the fish get too dark to continue grilling, finish cooking it in a 350° F. oven. Brush with glaze on both sides before serving.

GRILLED CATFISH WITH RED BEAN SALSA

6 servings

Salsa:

2/3 cup red beans, washed	1 jalapeno pepper, split, seeded
3 cups unsalted chicken broth	pinch of thyme, marjoram, gr. ginger
1/2 medium onion, whole	1 clove garlic, mashed
1 small carrot, peeled, whole	1 Tbsp cilantro, chopped

In a pot cover the beans with the broth, bring to a boil, cook 10 minutes and remove from stove. Allow to stand one hour. Place beans back on the stove, add all ingredients in the left column. As the vegetables get cooked, remove them and set aside. Cook the beans to very tender and with very little liquid remaining in the pot. Drain them and allow them to cool a little.

While the beans are cooking, impale the bell pepper on a fork and, over open flame, blacken the skin. Then place in a plastic bag and seal it, allowing the pepper to sweat for a few minutes. Rinse the skin off the pepper, remove seeds and dice it. Also dice the vegetables that cooked with the beans. Now add all salsa components together.

To cook the fish:

6 catfish fillets, skinless, 6-8 oz each	salt and pepper
2 Tbsp vegetable oil	3 Tbsp bread crumbs

Season the fillets, oil on both sides, and sprinkle lightly with bread crumbs. Grill over a medium hot grill (see grilling fish).To serve, place a bank of salsa on a plate, lean fish against it.

Serve with a cucumber or tomato salad (see recipes). This recipe may seem too time-consuming, but it is worth it! The salsa can be prepared a day in advance. Don't worry about the beans talking behind your back -- that's part of the fun!

SPECKLED (OR SHOULD I SAY SPECTACULAR?) TROUT FISHING IN QUEBEC

In 1954 I was a chef in a small, year round resort in the Laurentian mountains. Besides the main lodge and cabins, the resort owned and operated five hunting and fishing camps to which they flew their clients with sea planes. Besides preparing food at the lodge, I also had to plan meals and send food to the camps. I got to know the cooks and the native guides who worked there. They drew for me maps showing how I could approach some of the lakes by car over treacherous logging roads and then a long hike on foot, following blazed trails. If there were guests in the camps, I had to be careful not to show myself. The guests were told these places were only accessible by plane and they would wonder where I came from, since they did not hear a plane land.

The fishing was fabulous. The limit on speckled trout in Quebec at that time was 50 trout or 15 pounds, whichever came first! One time, I started fishing at 7 AM, and by 11 AM the bottom of my canoe was covered with speckled trout. I decided to take a count, since I was fishing in a Provincial Park and at the highway entrance I could be stopped at a road block and my creel checked. I was already one fish over the limit. Those days I received all my meals at the hotel, so I always gave my catch to the parents of my future wife to feed their family.

BROILED WHITEFISH WITH HORSERADISH MERINGUE

6 servings

6 portions of whitefish, boneless,

skin on, about 8 oz each

2 Tbsp vegetable oil

4 egg whites

1/3 cup, prepared horseradish, squeezed dry (in a cloth)

1/2 cup drained yogurt

salt and pepper

Preheat oven to 400° F. Preheat a broiler also. Place the fish skin down on a sheet pan, brush with oil and season it. Place it under a hot broiler for three to four minutes, remove. In a bowl whip egg whites and horseradish to stiff but not dry. Add the yogurt to it and fold to a smooth consistency. Do not over mix.

Mound this meringue evenly over the whitefish pieces, covering the whole surface.

Place it immediately in the oven for about 10 minutes (depending on thickness of the fish) to finish cooking. Transfer to warm plates.

Serve with boiled or mashed potatoes and a simple vegetable or salad.

This is both a healthy and quite tasty dish.

SAUTÉED PIKE WITH ANCHOVY BUTTER

Fillet, bone and skin the pike. Cut it into serving portions. Chop a little parsley.

For each portion mash 1 anchovy fillet with 1 Tbsp butter to a smooth paste. Preheat a suitable pan. Season the pike with salt and pepper and dust it with flour. Then, sauté it in butter.

Transfer cooked pike to plates, sprinkle with lemon juice, spoon anchovy butter over and top with chopped parsley. Serve with boiled potatoes and a simple vegetable or a salad.

P.S. You may also grill the pike.

SIMPLE FISH STIR-FRY

6 servings

Read stir-frying instructions on page....

6 cups assorted vegetables in bite size pieces such as: asparagus, broccoli florets and peeled stems, scallions, pea pods, water chestnuts, bok-choy, napa, red and yellow bell peppers, zucchini, summer squash, mushrooms, etc.

36 oz fish cut into 2 inch long strips (small, finger thick)	1/2 tsp red pepper flakes
peanut or canola oil as needed	1/3 cup imported soy sauce
2 Tbsp chopped garlic	1 Tbsp corn starch dissolved in
2 Tbsp grated fresh ginger	3 Tbsp sherry wine

Cook the fish first, then the vegetables with garlic and ginger. After the vegetables turn bright in color and are heated through, add the starch with wine and stir to thicken. Fold in the cooked fish. Serve immediately over steamed rice (see recipe) or plain noodles.

BOHEMIAN FISH SOUP

6 servings

The Czechs and Germans traditionally serve this soup at Christmas time. It is made from the heads and bones of carp. In Europe, the carp are raised in ponds, and then placed in floating wooden crates in rivers, where the fish purge themselves. Carp there has a very good taste, similar to our whitefish and is served in the finest restaurants. I have tried to eat carp in this country and Canada, but found the odor bad. So instead of carp, we shall use the heads and bones of other fresh water fish, such as whitefish, pike or walleyes. Saltwater fish also make very good soup, with the exception of salmon.

Always remove the gills before cooking, as they would turn the broth bitter. If the fish had roe (females) or milt (sperm sacks of the males), add them to the soup also. They taste great!

Stock:

1 small carrot, chopped	20 bruised peppercorns
1 branch of celery	1/2 cup butter
1 bay leaf	2 lbs of fish heads and bones, washed
1 small onion, chopped	1/2 cup dry white wine
1 tsp dry thyme	1 cup clam juice
1 small leek, white part only	1/2 Tbsp salt, water

In a stainless sauce pan sweat vegetables in butter, then add fish heads and bones. Add wine, clam juice and seasoning and enough water to not quite cover the bones. Bring to a low simmer, cook 20 minutes and strain. Pluck the meat off the heads, reserve (separately) with stock.

While stock is cooking, prepare the garnish.

Garnish:

1/2 cup each: carrots, celery and leeks cut into a matchstick-sized julienne. Once fish stock is ready, cook the garnish to tender in a small amount of the stock. Set aside.

Final preparation:

1/2 stick of butter	1/2 cup heavy cream
4 Tbsp flour	

Melt butter, add flour. Cook 2 minutes without browning. Whip in 5 cups of the cool fish stock, bring to a boil. Cook 10 minutes. Add cream, garnish, and the meat picked off the heads and bones. Taste and adjust seasoning.

INEDIBLE FISH?

When someone tells me that something is not good to eat (see Jack rabbit story), I want to know why. Quite often people just do not know how to prepare it or are turned off by the appearance of it. This could be the case with eel, which is highly valued in Europe and tastes excellent. I have never eaten lampreys, but heard that they are also very good.

The Orientals, some of whom have subsisted on fish for millennia, value fish heads much more than fillets. In Malayan and Thai restaurants, a fish head is the most expensive item on the menu. The Inuit eat the fish heads and feed the bodies to their sled dogs. When bears have an abundance of salmon, they eat the heads and skins, leaving the bodies to rot. Caviar is raw fish roe, a delicacy. The sperm is also very good to eat!

Fishing a small inland lake I had a strike and a hard fighting fish was on my line. Thinking I had a nice big bass, I was surprised to land a beautiful green dog fish. Having heard it was not edible, I wanted to find out why. Nobody seemed to know. So at home I filleted it and placed in a skillet to sauté it for dinner. After a few minutes I was shocked to see it turn into a peanut butter consistency and smelling horrible. I had my answer! A similar experience came with a freshwater shad I caught while fishing for walleyes in an Ontario river. Other than that, a sheepshead did not impress me either and the local carp, even if they came from a pristine lake, smelled and tasted bad.

In the ocean there are several species which, in times of plenty high-quality fish, used to be considered trash. They are now sold commercially. Some look horrendous when alive. Nothing is underutilized any more. Almost anything can be made into fish sticks or cakes.

Then there are beautiful fish, which for various reasons are not edible or do not keep well or are even poisonous.

BROILED FLOUNDER (OR) SOLE FILLETS

4 servings

1 1/2 lbs fillets

4 Tbsp melted butter

salt, pepper, paprika

2 Tbsp bread crumbs

Preheat a broiler. Dip the fillets in melted butter to coat both sides. Place them on a cookie sheet, sprinkle lightly with salt, pepper, paprika and bread crumbs. Place them 1 1/2 inches from the heating element and brown quickly. Thin fillets will be cooked in about 3 minutes. With a wide spatula, transfer them to warm plates.

Serve with fresh vegetables and boiled potatoes.

Filleting FlatFish

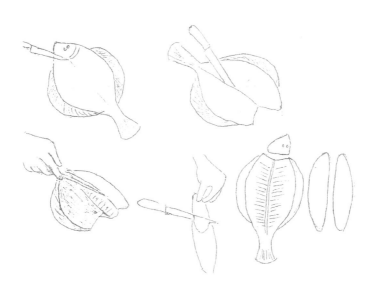

1. Cut head off.

2. Cut along the lateral (center) line to the spine.

3. Slice one fillet off the bones.

4. Follow with the other fillet (Flat fish have 4 fillets)

5. Turn fish over and repeat on the other side.

6. To skin them, place fillets skin side down and holding skin at the tail end, Slide knife between skin and flesh

FLOUNDER FILLETS SAUTÉED WITH BROWN BUTTER AND CAPERS

4 servings

1 1/2 lbs flounder fillets	2 Tbsp lemon juice
flour for dusting	1 Tbsp chopped parsley
4 Tbsp canola oil	3 Tbsp capers, rinsed
1/3 cup butter	salt and pepper

Preheat 2 large skillets. Season the flounder and dredge in flour. Shake excess off. Add oil to pans, place fillets in. Brown quickly on one side, turn over and finish on the other side. Transfer to plates. Add butter to one of the pans and brown. Quickly add the lemon juice, capers and parsley, swirl around and spoon over the fish.

Serve with potatoes and a simple vegetable or a salad.

GRILLED GROUPER WITH CORN SALSA

6 servings

Six 7-8 oz portions of grouper fillet

salt, pepper, vegetable oil, bread crumbs

Salsa:

Kernels cut from 1 ear of fresh corn, brought to a boil in 1/4 cup of water and drained.

1 ripe avocado, mashed	juice of 2 limes
zest of 1/2 lime, finely grated	1 Tbsp chopped cilantro leaves
Tabasco to taste	1 Tbsp olive oil
1/2 tsp garlic, mashed	salt and pepper
1 cup seeded and diced tomatoes	

In a bowl mix everything together, refrigerate 2 hours before serving. Allow it to return to room temperature for service. This could be made even a day in advance.

To cook the fish: preheat a grill or a heavy (preferably cast iron) skillet. Season the fish with salt and pepper, brush with oil, sprinkle lightly with bread crumbs.

Oil the grill and place the fish on over medium fire. If using a pan, omit bread crumbs and leave the pan dry. Grill the fish approximately 5 minutes per side, depending on thickness.

Serve bordered with salsa and some new potatoes.

Note: If the fish gets too dark to continue grilling, finish cooking it in a 350° F. oven.

Firm fleshed and oily fish are best suited for grilling. To grill thin or crumbly fillets, place them in a grilling basket (flat wire basket with hinged lid) and use a hot fire (see directions at the start). Small fish are best grilled whole; you may easily skin and bone them after grilling

(see grilling fish above). Adding water-soaked hardwood chips to the coals will give the fish a mild smoky flavor.

POMPANO IN PARCHMENT

6 servings

6 sheets of parchment, about 12"x 22"

2 Tbsp vegetable oil

6 pompano, about 10-12 oz each, headless, gutted, fins trimmed

salt, pepper

2 cups combined: finely shredded

carrots, celery and white part of leek.

1/2 cup combined: chopped parsley, chives, dill, tarragon

1 Tbsp lemon zest, finely grated

3 Tbsp lemon juice

1 cup sliced mushrooms

Preheat oven to 400° F. Fold the parchment paper in halves. Trace half of a heart (teardrop shape) on it, going all the way to the edges with the straight side on the fold. Cut these out with scissors. Open up and brush the inside with oil. Season the pompano with salt and pepper, place on one half of the parchment heart. Put the rest of the ingredients into a bowl and mix to disperse evenly. Divide this mixture over the fish.

Fold the other half of the paper over the fish. The parchment, when closed over the fish,

has to be wide enough so that you still have at least one inch of overlap beyond the fish all around the open side.

Starting at the rounded end of the opening, fold over a small part of the overlap, then continue folding the edge, always overlapping and pressing the previous fold, all around the fish until you reach the point. Twist and fold the point under. The fish should now be sealed in the parchment. Brush the top with the remaining oil.

To bake:

Place the wrapped fish on a sheet pan and bake in the oven approx.15-18 minutes, depending on the thickness of the fish. If properly wrapped, the parchment should inflate like a balloon.

Serve the fish in parchment to the guests, then cut the pouch open and slide the fish out onto the plate. Discard the paper.

Serve with simple potatoes or French bread and a salad.

BAKED STUFFED FLOUNDER WITH CRABMEAT

6 servings

Besides flounder, any small fish fillets, even thin slices of large fish, can be used.

In this recipe we use skinless and boneless fillets, which are easier to handle.

12 flounder fillets, about 2 1/2 oz each

bread crumbs melted butter salt paprika

Filling:

1/2 cup mayonnaise	dash of cayenne pepper
3 Tbsp sour cream	2 cups crabmeat
1/4 cup chopped scallions	1 tsp lemon juice
1 Tbsp Dijon mustard	salt to taste
1 hard-boiled egg, chopped	

Preheat oven to 400° F.

In a bowl mix the first six ingredients of the filling together. Pick the crabmeat over to remove shell and cartilage fragments. If it has been frozen, squeeze excess juice out. Chop any large chunks up, then stir all ingredients together.

Assembly:

Brush a baking sheet with butter. Dip 6 flounder fillets in crumbs on one side, place crumbed side down on the baking sheet. Mound filling on top of these fillets, distributing evenly. Cut 2 1/2 inch slits lengthwise through the centers of the remaining fillets, leaving both ends connected. Drape these fillets over the stuffing, aligning them with the bottoms, keeping the slits open to expose the stuffing. Brush top fillets with melted butter, sprinkle lightly with salt and paprika.

The flounders may be prepared this way far in advance, and then refrigerated for later use.

To bake:

Bake the flounders approx. 18 minutes to cook the fish and heat the stuffing through. Use a large, wide spatula to transfer them to serving plates.

Serve with simple potatoes and a vegetable or salad.

BAKED STUFFED FLOUNDER WITH SHRIMP MOUSSELINE IN PHYLO, SHRIMP SAUCE.

8 servings

This is an elegant dish, but not very difficult to produce. You may use various types of fish, either small fillets or slices of a larger fish. Some prior culinary experience helps.

Mousseline filling:

1 1/2 cups peeled and deveined raw shrimp (save the shells)

1/2 cup (total) chopped: parsley, dill, tarragon, chives. Save herb stems.

1 egg white	1 Tbsp cider vinegar
salt and white pepper to taste	3/4 cup heavy cream

Place all ingredients except herbs in a processor and puree smooth .Fold in herbs and refrigerate.

Sauce:

1 qt raw shrimp shells	1 cup clam juice
3 Tbsp clarified butter	1 Tbsp starch
1 Tbsp shallots, finely chopped	2 Tbsp water
herb stems	1/4 cup softened butter
1 cup dry white wine	

Preheat oven to 400° F. In a stainless saucepan sauté shrimp shells in clarified butter to coat well, and then place in the oven. Roast, stirring once a while, about 18-20 minutes, until shells get a bronze tint. Remove pan from oven, stir in shallots and herb stems, add wine and clam juice. Bring to a simmer, cook 20 min. and strain into a small stainless saucepan . Discard shells. Put juice back on stove, reduce by boiling to 1 cup. Mix starch with water, stir in to thicken. With a wire whisk, whip in the butter. Keep sauce warm, covered.

Final assembly (you can work on this while the sauce is cooking):

Eight 4 oz slices of halibut (or small fillets of other fish), 1/3 inch thick, skinless

1/2 cup clarified butter (see Basic Fish Cooking Methods - Deep Frying) or olive oil

8 sheets of (preferably fresh) phyllo dough

Spread halibut slices on a clean surface, season lightly with salt & pepper. Mound the shrimp mousseline on them, dividing equally. Roll the slices up, encasing the filling. Set aside.

Lightly brush a sheet of phyllo with butter or oil. Cover with another sheet, repeat.

Fold it in half, brush again. Set a halibut bundle at one narrow end and roll up, wrapping it up snugly in the phyllo, distributing the wrap evenly around the fish.

Place it seam side down on a parchment-covered baking sheet and brush top with butter.

Repeat, using up all the fish. You may refrigerate the halibut at this point to bake later, but do not keep it overnight, as the dough will turn soggy.

To bake:

Preheat oven to 400° F. Space the bundles about 2 inches apart, bake approximately 18 minutes to brown the outside and to an internal temperature of 120° F.

To serve: spoon sauce on warm plates, place fish on top. Serve with a simple vegetable, crispy hot rolls and a salad.

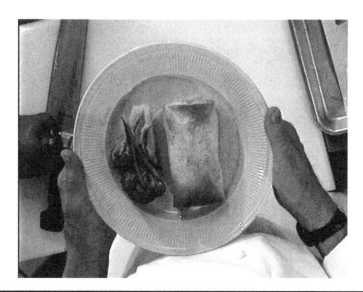

STRIPED BASS SAUTÉED WITH MUSHROOM, TOMATOES AND OLIVES

6 servings

6 portions of bass, 6-8 oz each

flour

4 Tbsp butter

3 Tbsp onion, chopped

3 cups fresh mushrooms, sliced

2 cups seeded, diced tomatoes

1/2 cup pitted oil cured (Moroccan) olives

2 Tbsp chopped parsley

juice of 1 lemon

salt, pepper

Preheat 2 large skillets. Season the bass, dust with flour. Sauté the bass in the butter to brown on both sides. If the pieces are thick, either put a lid on after you have turned the fish over and lower the temperature, or place uncovered pans in a 350° F. oven to finish cooking.

Place cooked bass on plates. To the same skillet add the onions and mushrooms, sauté for 1 minute, then add tomatoes, olives, parsley and lemon juice. Heat through and spoon over fish.

DOVER SOLE MURAT

4 servings

2 whole Dover sole, 20 oz each, skinned, filleted and cut into small finger-sized strips

milk to dip the strips in

1/2 cup peanut oil

1/2 cup olive oil for frying

Seasoned flour for coating:

(Use for any sautéed fish)

Sift together twice:

1 cup flour

2 Tbsp paprika

1 tsp salt

1/2 tsp white pepper

Garnish:

1/2 lb mushrooms, quartered

1 Tbsp chopped shallots

2 Tbsp butter

1 1/2 Tbsp lemon juice

2 Tbsp sherry wine

1 tsp Worcestershire sauce

1 bay leaf

1 small chili pepper, crushed

1 cup cooked, quartered baby artichokes

1/2 cup chicken stock

pinch of sugar

Sauté mushrooms and shallots in butter without browning. Add liquids and seasoning, bring to a boil, reduce to 1/2 cup of liquid remaining. Add the artichokes, set aside.

Final preparation:

Dip sole in milk, dredge in seasoned flour - shake excess off. In a large pan, preheat oils (about 1/2 inch deep).Add sole in batches, sauté to golden brown on all sides. Lift them out with a skimmer or a slotted spoon and drain well.

Place cooked sole in another skillet, pour garnish over. Toss gently and serve.

Note: Sautéed potatoes and tomatoes are sometimes added.

DIFFERENT TASTES, DIFFERENT CUSTOMS

Depending on where we are born, we are all made to believe that certain foods are good or bad, according to prevailing local customs. Much of it, passed on from generation to generation is falsehood. Television and air travel has opened our eyes to uncommon foods consumed in various parts of the world, some of which we may have previously considered "bad". If we are willing to sample different dishes with open mind, we can be pleasantly surprised.

If you visit an Oriental market, you will see live animals on display. Customers make a selection, after which the vendor kills and preps it on the spot in minutes.

In some places, restaurants have sets of aquariums featuring various live fish. Guests, accompanied by a waiter, select their dinner from them, prepared while they wait.

They love the idea of getting a very fresh fish to eat.

In front of groceries, you may see containers with rice, beans and dried beetles, which are a common flavoring condiment. Fishermen in sampans pull up octopi caught in ceramic traps. The most important thing for them is, that when emptying the trap, the octopus lands on the floor the right side up, otherwise, according to superstition, the sampan might perish in the next storm on the sea. Then they chop up the wiggling octopus with their cleavers into bite size pieces and eat it like candy.

To many Orientals, fish heads are a delicacy, selling for perhaps three times as much as fillets of the same fish. While visiting Singapore I stayed in the Mandarin hotel. They had French, Italian, Mandarin and Malayan dining rooms. Always interested to learn about different cuisines, I chose the Malayan dining room for my lunch one day.

I soon realized I was the only *round eye* in the room. Looking over the menu, I chose the most expensive item – Curried Fish Head. The shocked waiter asked: "Are you sure you want that?" When I said yes, he stood there, perhaps expecting me to start laughing, admitting I was only joking. Then he repeated the question. I could only presume that he never had a *round eye* customer order a fish head. I inquired whether it was very spicy. He assured me it was mild.

A large fist size head came floating in a pool of sauce, the surface of which was covered with tiny red and green peppers. I assumed the peppers were viciously hot, so I scooped them up and put them in an empty dish. A large mound of steamed rice came on the side. I did not expect to be able to eat all of it, but I did! It was very delicious. Some people have asked me: "What do you eat on a fish head?"

The simple answer is - everything but the bones!

SEARED TUNA LOIN, ORIENTAL SAUCE

Serve as a first course (15 or more appetizer size servings)

Note: For those who refuse to eat sushi or sashimi, this recipe is not for you. Well-done tuna is very dry and unpleasant to eat. Rare tuna will melt in your mouth.

2 1/4 lb trimmed, skinless tuna loin, dark strip removed, cut into 3 inch thick cylinders.

Sauce:

1/2 cup peanut or canola oil	2 tsp fresh ginger, grated
1/2 Tbsp light soy sauce	1 tsp garlic, mashed
1 tsp Malayan chili sauce	pinch of salt
1 1/2 Tbsp red wine vinegar	1 lime zest, finely grated
1 1/2 tsp sugar	juice of 1 1/2 limes
2 Tbsp ketchup	

Blend sauce ingredients together. Set aside.

Searing spices:

2 Tbsp paprika	1 tsp cayenne
1 Tbsp cumin	1 Tbsp dry tarragon
1 Tbsp dry mustard	1 Tbsp dry thyme

Blend these spices in a shallow dish.

Final preparation:

2 Tbsp peanut oil

Preheat a dry, large skillet or a sizzling platter to smoking hot.

Season the tuna with salt and roll it in the spice blend. Add the 2 Tbsp oil to the hot pan, place tuna in. Sear over high heat to blacken on all sides.

Remove it from the pan and wrap it snugly in plastic wrap.

To serve:

Using a sharp, thin-bladed knife, slice the wrapped tuna through the plastic into 1/3" thick slices. Then peel the wrap off. Spill some sauce on plates, arrange the slices (overlapping each other) on top of sauce.

SEAFOOD ALA NAGE (LITERALLY "IN THE SWIM")

6 servings

Just about all the components of this classical French dish can be prepared well in advance. In the last ½ hour, all you would have to do is poach the fish and serve it! Don't forget the bread.

This recipe is similar to the Bouillabaisse, in which the fish is served on soup plates in the broth. Various firm-fleshed fish, singly or in combinations, may be used, plus shellfish and crustaceans.

We just have to be mindful that, depending on the size of the pieces, and their nature, some fish will take more time than others to cook. A kind of garlic-flavored mayonnaise, called *"aioli"*, is traditionally served with it.

6 3 oz servings of firm-fleshed boneless and skinless fish

18 raw shrimp, 16-20 size, peeled and deveined

18 sea scallops

You may also use mussels, clams, crabs and even lobsters.

Fish stock:

2 lb lean fish bones and heads

1 cup onions, sliced

1 qt water

1/2 bay leaf

1/2 cup cider vinegar

few parsley stems

1/2 cup dry white wine

pinch of thyme

1/4 cup white of leek, sliced

1/2 tsp crushed peppercorns

1/3 cup carrots, sliced

2 slices of lemon

2 Tbsp salt

Remove gills from heads, wash all in cold water. Place it in a stainless pot with the rest of the ingredients, bring to a simmer. Cook 20 minutes and strain through a cloth. Keep warm. While the stock is cooking, cut the vegetables for garnish.

Vegetable garnish:

1/4 cup carrots, cut into 1/3 inch size dice

1/4 cup leek, cut into 1/3 inch size dice

1/4 cup celery, cut into 1/3 inch size dice

1/4 cup peeled, diced tomato

2 Tbsp chopped parsley

Cook carrots, leeks and celery in the fish stock to tender, drain and reserve. Peel and dice the tomato, set aside. Set parsley aside. Next make the aioli.

Aioli:

1 tsp lemon juice

2 egg yolks

1/2 tsp Dijon mustard

pinch of salt

1 cup olive oil

10 large garlic cloves, mashed

Have all ingredients at room temperature. Place lemon juice, yolks, mustard and salt into a blender. With machine running, start adding oil a little at a time, until it is incorporated and emulsified. Add garlic last. Cover and set aside.

Final preparation:

Taste the fish stock and adjust seasoning as needed. 20 minutes before serving: Reheat bread baguettes in 350° F. oven.

In a wide, stainless saucepan bring the stock to a boil. Reduce heat to just warm. Drop the fin-fish in, making sure they are separated in the stock. Keep stock temp at 185° F. 5 minutes later, drop the shrimp and scallops in. Shake pan. Maintain the stock temperature at 185° F. for 3 minutes more. Add the vegetable garnish.

Divide fish between plates, add stock, sprinkle with parsley.

Serve with aioli and hot French bread on the side, along with soup spoons as well as forks. Guests either dip fish pieces in the aioli or put dabs of it on the fish.

OVEN-POACHED STRIPED BASS, TARRAGON SAUCE

6 servings

2 Tbsp softened butter	1/2 cup dry vermouth
6 bass fillets, 7 oz each	1/2 cup dry white wine
3 shallots, chopped finely	1 cup clam juice
juice of 1/2 lemon	1 cup heavy cream
salt, white pepper	3 Tbsp fresh tarragon, chopped fine

Preheat oven to 325° F. Butter the bottom of a 3 inch deep dish (ceramic, Pyrex, stainless) large enough to hold the fish in one layer, without crowding. Sprinkle with shallots, place fish in skin down. Sprinkle with lemon juice, season lightly with salt and pepper.

In a saucepan bring wines and clam juice to a boil, then pour over the fish. Cover and place it in the oven. Cook about 10 minutes, depending on thickness of the fish.

With a spatula, carefully lift the fish out and place on a warm platter. Cover it and keep warm. Strain the juice back into the saucepan and on a hot stove boil to reduce to 1/2 cup. Add the cream and again reduce, this time to a sauce consistency. Stir in the tarragon, taste and adjust seasoning.

Peel skin off fish, place on warm plates and spoon sauce over. Serve with potatoes, steamed rice (see recipe) or French bread and some simple salad or vegetable.

POACHED BLUEFISH

6 servings

Because of high oil content and strong taste, bluefish is best prepared poached or grilled.

In this recipe, we cook it in a broth called "Court Bouillon." Any fish will stay moister and hold together better if we leave the skin on for cooking. We can peel it off easily after cooking.

Court Bouillon:

2 qts water	1/2 small onion, sliced
1 bay leaf	2 Tbsp salt
1/2 cup cider vinegar	1/2 lemon, sliced
1 Tbsp peppercorns	melted butter
1/2 small carrot, sliced	10 parsley stems
1/2 tsp thyme	lemon wedges

In a stainless pot bring everything to a boil, cook it 15 minutes and then strain. Place the fish in a pan wide and deep enough to hold it in one layer, without crowding. Pour the hot bouillon over to completely cover the fish, shake the pan to make sure it is not stuck to the bottom, place pan on low heat and hold at a temperature of 180° F. for approximately 15 minutes, depending on thickness of the fish.

Lift cooked fish out to a platter, transfer to plates. Serve with lemon and melted butter, or some salsa (see recipes) on the side, boiled potatoes and a salad.

OVEN STEAMED FILLETS

with Mussels and Chives

6 servings

Many different types of ocean fish can be used in this recipe.

1 1/2 cups dry white wine	24 mussels, washed
20 parsley stems (no leaves)	buttered parchment paper
2 Tbsp finely cut chives	3 large or 6 small fish fillets
2 bay leaves	salt and white pepper
pinch of thyme	2 egg yolks
4 shallots, chopped fine	1 cup heavy cream

Preheat oven to 350° F. In a stainless saucepan bring wine, shallots and herbs to a boil. Add mussels, cover tightly and place on high heat, shaking pan occasionally. As soon as mussels open (3 minutes), take them out with a slotted spoon. Remove them from shells, de-beard, cover and keep warm. Strain juice through a cloth, keep hot.

Select a suitable non-aluminum pan to cook the fillets in one layer. Cover bottom with buttered parchment paper, place fish in, pour mussel juice over and add a touch of salt. Cover pan and place in the oven for about 15 minutes. Lift fillets out, and place on warm serving plates. Cover and keep warm.

Pour juice from soles into a saucepan, reduce by fast boiling to 1/2 cup. In a bowl mix yolks with cream, slowly pour hot juice in, mix and return to saucepan. Stir over medium heat **until sauce coats spoon**. DO NOT BOIL!

Place mussels on soles, spoon sauce over, sprinkle with chives.

Serve with boiled potatoes or steamed rice (see recipe).

STEAMED RED SNAPPER IN THE CHINESE MANNER

6 servings

While traveling in Singapore and Bangkok, I sampled steamed fish in local restaurants and found it quite delicious. While you can steam cut fish portions, you may also serve small whole fish, such as snapper, grouper, black bass, pompano, butterfish, etc.

The fish should be scaled, gutted and gills removed. The head is left on, unless your guests would object to it (the Orientals consider the head the best part). Thick fish should be scored (vertical slits cut into the back 1 inch apart). Prepare sauce while the fish is steaming.

Figure 12-14 oz per person of whole, gutted fish, with head on.

To steam:

1/2 cup sherry wine	1/2 cup carrots, cut into fine threads
1 Tbsp finely grated fresh ginger	1/2 cup celery, cut into fine threads
1 tsp finely sliced Jalapeno pepper	1 Tbsp chopped garlic

Prepare a steamer with a tight-fitting lid. Place 1/2 inch of boiling water in the bottom.

Rub fish inside and out with sherry, place them in one layer, without crowding into the steamer.

Mix vegetables with garlic and ginger, spread evenly over fish. Cover the steamer tightly and steam 7-10 minutes, depending on the thickness of the fish.

At home, you may serve the whole fish as it is customary in the Far East. If you have finicky eaters or small children, you may want to debone the fish. To do so, place the fish on a tray. Break off the head and pull out the fins. With a table knife, separate the upper fillet into lateral halves along the visible line. First push the back half off to the side, then slide the belly part off the rib cage. Now pick up the spine at the tail and with the rib cage connected, lift it up and remove.

The fish should be boneless now. Place the clean lower fillet on a serving plate, then reassemble the upper fillet on top to its original position. Rearrange cooked vegetables over fish.

Sauce:

1/3 cup scallions, finely sliced	zest of 1/2 lemon, grated
juice of 1/2 lemon	1/2 cup med. dry sherry wine
1 tsp sugar	1/4 tsp dark sesame oil
1/3 cup light soy sauce	

Warm sauce ingredients together, spoon over fish. Serve with steamed rice (see recipe) and a salad.

STRIPED BASS CUTLETS

with dry Vermouth and Gremolata.

6 servings

36 oz striped bass fillets	zest of 1 lemon, grated finely
3 Tbsp butter	1 Tbsp lemon juice
salt & pepper	1 Tbsp Dijon mustard
1/2 cup dry vermouth	2 Tbsp chopped capers
2 Tbsp butter	3 Tbsp chopped parsley
2 Tbsp chopped shallots	

Filet, completely debone and skin a nice large bass. Cut it on an angle into 1/3 inch thick cutlets.

Have all ingredients ready at hand. Preheat 2 large non-stick skillets. Divide the 3 Tbsp butter between them and place the cutlets in without overlapping. Sprinkle lightly with salt and pepper, cover with lids and cook over medium-high heat 2-3 minutes, just to firm the cutlets up.

Using a large spatula, transfer them to warm plates. Pour vermouth into skillets, bring to a boil, combine into one pan. Whip in the remaining butter and rest of ingredients, spoon over fish.

Serve with boiled potatoes and a simple vegetable or a salad.

SALMON

Wild Atlantic salmon has become a thing of the past. There are not many surviving and we have no commercial fishing for them. There are five species of Pacific salmon. These are the King, Silver, Sockeye, Pink and Chum. Of those, the first three are sold in stores during the short fishing seasons assigned to the species. Pink salmon and Chum are mostly canned. Kings and Silvers have a fairly high fat content; Sockeyes are beautifully red, but fairly dry. Wild salmon have undoubtedly much better flavor than farm-raised. Large, ocean run Steelhead (also called Rainbow trout) is, when in season, available wild; the rest of the year it is farmed. Their taste and texture is very similar to salmon. Pacific steelhead's flesh is pink, as they feed on crustaceans. Lake and river sport-caught salmon and steelhead's flesh is beige. Farmed salmon always come from the Atlantic stock, regardless where the farm is located. They became a very popular fish. Their quality varies, depending on the type of feed and the site's water quality.

To Fillet a Larger Fish

1. Make an incision under the pectoral fin to the spine.

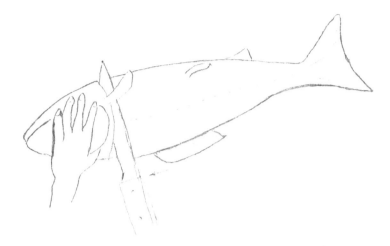

2. Turn the knife blade horizontal, touching the spine. With your free hand, hold belly flap up. With a sawing motion, cut top fillet off.

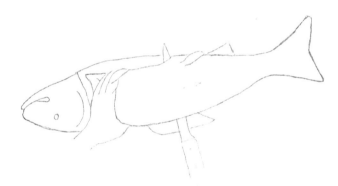

3. Turn fish over. Using the same technique, cut other fillet off just above the spine.

4. Slide the blade of the knife under the rib bones. Holding the edge of the knife against the bones, slice them off. Next trim the lower edge of the belly and the anal fin off. Remove remnants of dorsal fin.

5. Skin the fillets. With your free hand grasp the tail, then insert the knife at the tail between the flesh and the skin. Holding the blade slightly angled toward the skin, slice the skin off.

6. Removing pin bones.

On some fish, such as salmon, lake trout, whitefish and most ocean fish you can pull the remaining pin bones using needle nose pliers.

Pin bones of pike, walleye and shad have to be removed by carefully slicing around them.

POACHED SALMON

Whether you want to poach a whole fish, a side (boneless fillet, skin on) or individual portions, you will need enough court bouillon (the liquid) to cover the fish. In either case, you will also need a suitable, non-aluminum pan to accommodate the fish, without crowding. For a whole salmon it is best to have a fish poacher that you may purchase at a specialty cook's store. It is best to poach fish with skin on. You can peel it off easily after cooking.

Court bouillon for 6 individual portions or a whole side of salmon. For a whole 8 lb fish, double the recipe)

2 qts water

15 parsley stems (no leaves)

1 bottle dry white wine (or 1/2 cup cider vinegar)

1 tsp thyme

1 med. onion, sliced

2 Tbsp peppercorns

1 branch celery, sliced

3 Tbsp salt

1 lemon, sliced

In a stainless pot bring everything to a boil. Cook 20 minutes and strain through a cloth.

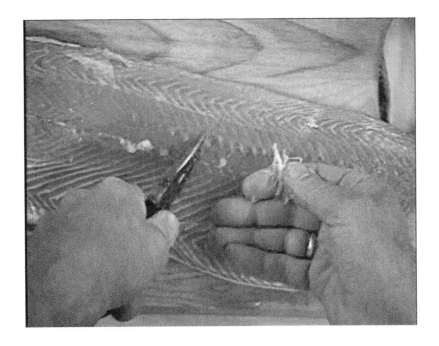

To cook the salmon:

For individual portions: Place the fish in a large, wide stainless saucepan in one layer, not crowded. Pour the hot court bouillon over; shake pan to make sure the fish is not stuck to the bottom. Place pan on a low heat, uncovered and monitor the temperature of the bouillon, making sure it never exceeds 180° F.

One inch thick fillet or steak will take approximately 12-15 minutes, thinner ones less time. To check for doneness, slide a spatula half way under a fillet, lift the center of the salmon and peek into the crack. When opaque, the fish is cooked. A slightly underdone salmon will be very moist to eat. Overcooking will result in dryness.

To test doneness of a salmon steak, insert a kitchen fork into the spine and try to lift the bones out. If done, they will come out easily. Carefully lift the portions out, drain and place on serving plates. Slide the tines of a table fork into the skin, and then peel it off, rolling it up on the fork like opening a can of sardines.

Serve with melted butter or some nice sauce, such as Hollandaise or dill. Accompany with boiled potatoes and a simple vegetable or salad.

Dill sauce (cold)**:**

pinch of salt and cayenne pepper	1/4 cup sour cream
1/2 cup mayonnaise	1 tsp Dijon mustard
1/2 cup finely chopped dill	

Stir all ingredients together. You may also make it in a blender. For a greener looking sauce, add a couple of spinach leaves to the blender.

NOTE: THE FOLLOWING IS MY FAVORITE RECIPE FOR LARGE PARTIES.

To poach a whole side of salmon (boneless fillet with skin on) which will be **served cold:** Place a sheet of parchment on the bottom of a suitable pan, large enough to hold it without bending the fish. Place the fish skin side down on it. Pour **boiling bouillon** over to completely cover the fish (make sure you have enough bouillon). Turn heat off. Cover pan tightly and hold warm (no heat underneath) until it cools down. When the temperature gets lukewarm, refrigerate. The next day, drain liquid off and discard. Using two large spatulas, lift fish out onto a carving board (if it sticks to the bottom, loosen it by placing the pan over heat for a few seconds).

To carve: using a sharp, thin-slicing knife, starting at the tail, slice the fish on an angle into 1/4 inch to 1/3 inch thick slices. Serve as a first course, light luncheon or appetizer, accompanied by garnishes such as tomato and hardboiled egg wedges, celery hearts, cucumber slices, scallions, radishes, potato salad, etc. and a cold sauce (see recipe above).

To poach a whole fish which is to be served cold, buffet style:

For appearance, it is best to leave the head and tail on. You need a large fish poacher (vessel).

Make the bouillon as above, then allow it to cool down. Lay the fish on its side on a rack inside the poacher, add the cool bouillon to cover the fish completely.

Place it on medium heat and gradually bring the temperature to 175° F., then lower the heat source to very low. If you put a lid on, be careful to monitor the temperature every few minutes, keeping it between 165° F. and 180° F. Poach it about 8 minutes per pound of fish.

After about 45 minutes of cooking, insert the thermometer into the thickest part of the fish and if not done, repeat in 7 minute intervals. When the fish temperature reaches 120° F., take it off the stove and allow it to cool down in the court bouillon. When cool, refrigerate it as it is in the liquid, covered.

Next day, lift the fish out of the bouillon, place it on a large platter and peel the skin off. Using a small knife, you may also scrape off the lateral line (brownish part running in the center, the length of the fish on both sides).

Decorate it to your liking, using sliced cucumbers, eggs or radishes to simulate scales.

To carve it, start at the head. Cut two inch wide pieces of the fish crossways and only half way down, until you reach the spine. Remove one piece at a time by inserting a knife horizontally into the back of the fish just above the spine and lifting the piece off the bones. When the upper fillet is all carved, remove the spine with the rib cage bones connected to it. To do that, starting at the tail, lift the spine up, then break it off at the head and discard. You may now carve the bottom fillet. Serve with dill sauce and garnish as in the recipe above.

Add hot crispy rolls or French bread and a nice dry white wine.

Boning a Whole Cooked Fish

1. With the fish laying on its side, split the upper fillet lengthwise along the lateral (center) line from head to tail allowing the knife to slide on top of the spine. With the blade of the knife push the upper half (the loin) of the fillet off the spine to the side

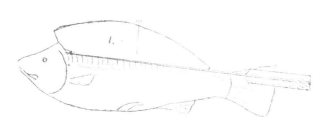

2. Now slide the lower (belly) part off the rib cage, being careful to leave all the bones connected to the spine. Remove all fins

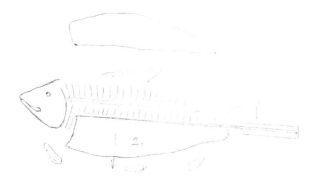

3. With your free hand, pick up the tail and with it lift the spine with the rib cage attached to it off the bottom fillet. If any meat sticks to the bones, free it using a table fork. Discard bones, head and fins.

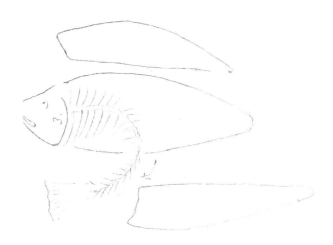

4. Using a large, wide spatula transfer fillets unto a clean plate or platter. Reassemble the two halves of the upper fillet into their original position.

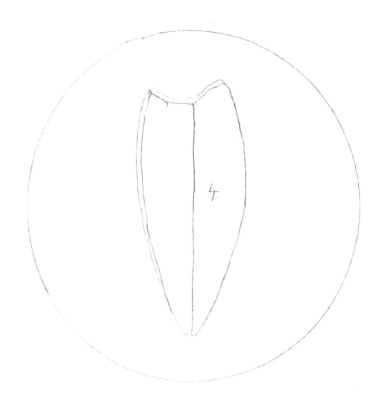

GRAVLAX

A Swedish delicacy, Gravlax is a salmon cured with salt and sugar, flavored with fresh dill and pepper and traditionally served with a sweet brown mustard. It is not cooked.

Use a very fresh saltwater salmon only. Fillet and bone it out completely, leaving the skin on.

For an 8 lb (whole weight) salmon, you will need:

1/2 cup Kosher salt

1/2 cup granulated sugar

3 Tbsp freshly cracked black pepper

1 cup (combined) chopped fresh herbs:

tarragon, lovage, chervil, parsley, dill

Spread a large piece of film wrap on a table. Place on it one of the salmon fillets, skin-side down. Sprinkle the fillet evenly with half of the salt, sugar and pepper. Spread the herbs over. Sprinkle the rest of the seasonings over the other fillet, place on top of the first one skin-side up. Snugly wrap the entire fish in the film and set it on a large tray.

Place it in a refrigerator, cover with another tray and weigh down with about a 5 lb object. Refrigerate, turning over daily, for 3 days.

To serve: Open the package, drain off any juice. Spread fillets apart, place skin-side down. Spread the herbs evenly over them. Using a sharp, thin, long-bladed slicing knife, start at the tail end. Cut very thin slices on a long angle and cut them off before reaching the skin. Try to keep a border of the herbs on top of each slice for flavor and appearance. Arrange them neatly on plates or a platter and sprinkle them with vinaigrette made of:

  1/2 cup good olive oil

  1/4 cup red wine vinegar

  1 tsp Dijon mustard

Serve gravlax as an appetizer, a first course, on canapés and sandwiches made with pumpernickel bread and cucumber slices, or as a part of a cold seafood plate.

SMOKING FISH

All proteins intended for smoking MUST BE CURED FIRST, to inhibit the growth of bacteria. We may either dry cure them or brine them. There are several methods of smoking fish, but we will be concerned with two:

Hot smoking, at temperatures above 120° F. and

Cold smoking, at temperatures below 90° F.

For the curing we use a non-iodized salt, such as pickling salt or Kosher salt. The cure (sodium nitrite and sodium nitrate) is sold in butcher supply stores.

HOT SMOKED FISH

When hot-smoking, the product is cooked in the smoker. We hot-smoke whitefish, lake, rainbow and speckled trout, carp, suckers, white bass, chubs, sturgeon, eel, etc.

Many ocean fish are also hot-smoked. Scaly fish should be scaled first, except very fine-scaled fish, such as speckled trout.

Small fish, such as brook trout, white bass, chubs or small suckers are left whole, only eviscerated. Medium size fish are split through the back and the two sides left connected at the belly, spine left in. We split large fish in halves lengthwise, remove the spine, but leave the rib cage and other bones in to protect the fish from drying out. We may also cut it into steaks.

To prepare the fish for brining:

Scrape out any blood and membrane from the cavity and wash the fish well. Make a solution of 2 cups of salt for every one gallon of room temperature water. Soak the fish in it for 30 minutes to leach out any blood. Drain and rinse.

Brine:

2 1/2 gals water at 90° F.	1 lb sugar
2 Tbsp thyme leaves	2 Tbsp crushed coriander
2 lb. salt (pickling or Kosher)	1 oz cure
1/4 cup bay leaves	

Prepare it in a non-corrosive (plastic, glass, etc.) container. You will need enough brine to completely immerse the fish, without crowding. The brine cannot be reused. Stir it well to dissolve sugar, salt and cure.

Immerse the fish in this brine for 1- 4 hours, depending on its size. Then rinse it with cold water and place on racks in a breezy, cold place to dry for at least 4 hours, preferably overnight.

The surface should develop a shiny coat called "pellicle". The pellicle protects the fish from drying out while smoking.

To smoke:

Place the fish in the smoker and smoke with a dense, but cool smoke (120° F. – 130° F.) for about six to eight hours, then increase the temperature to 150° F. for two hours. (Health authorities recommend higher temperatures).

NOTE: These times are APPROXIMATE ONLY! The length of smoking time depends mostly on the density of the smoke, how crowded the smoker is and the size of the product being smoked. You have to experiment and be the final judge. When done, the product should have a nice bronze tint and be cooked. (If there is any translucency or pinkness at the spine visible, return it to the smoker and increase the temperature, or finish in an oven).

Remove it from the smoker, wrap in paper (plastic wrap encourages mold growth) and refrigerate. Do not keep longer than one week refrigerated. To keep it longer, wrap snugly in plastic and freeze.

Serve with *Apple-horseradish* (see recipe) served as a relish on the side.

Note: See *"Cold-Smoked Salmon"* recipe below for smoker temperature control.

COLD - SMOKED SALMON

The characteristic of cold-smoked salmon (also called lox) is the pliable, moist texture suitable for thin slicing. The fish are always filleted for cold smoking, with skin left on. Other fish, such as lake trout or bluefish, can also be cold-smoked just like many meat products such as ham, bacon, pastrami, some sausages, etc. There is no reason to fear consuming fish that has not been cooked; curing replaces cooking. Many other products we eat are not cooked, such as pickled herring, ceviche, sashimi, sushi, salami, prosciutto and Westphalian ham among others.

To cold-smoke, care must be taken not to allow the temperature inside the smoker to rise above 90° F. There are several ways to accomplish this; the easiest is smoking during cold outside temperatures. Summer heat is our biggest enemy.

We can lower the smoker temperature by:

1. Smoking during the night, when the outside temperature drops.

2. Distancing the smoke generator from the smoke house. By placing the heating element which produces the smoke outside the smoker, we allow some heat to dissipate. The longer the distance we place it from the smoker, the cooler the smoke gets. The smoke has to be ducted into the smoker. The ducts can be chilled with ice or cold water.

3. Placing pans with ice in the smoker above and below the products being smoked.

4. Having the fish well-chilled (but NOT frozen) before placing it in the smoker and periodically removing and re-chilling it before returning to the smoker.

Simple dry cure for salmon and other fish:

Fillet and completely bone out the salmon, leaving the skin on. Weigh the fillets; write weight down. Take a large flat tray and sprinkle a 1/4 inch thick layer of Kosher or pickling salt on it. Then sprinkle 1/16 inch layer of sugar over the salt. Lay the salmon fillets skin-side down on top of this. Sprinkle them first with 1/16 inch of sugar, then with 1/4 inch of salt. Place another flat tray on top and weigh it down with an object about 8 lb. heavy. Set this in a cold room or a refrigerator.

Timing: Cure the fish about 2 hours per pound of fillet. As an example, fillets cut from an 8 lb salmon (weighing 3 1/2 lb each) will cure in about 7 hours. Over-curing will make the fish salty. Under-curing will cause softness in texture and the fish will spoil faster.

Rinse the cured fish with cold water, then pat dry with a paper towel. Place fillets skin-side down on wire racks in a cool, breezy place or a refrigerator overnight. When a shiny surface develops (called pellicle), the fish is ready for smoking.

To cold smoke: Place the cured fillets on a wire rack in the smoker or hang them on strings inserted near the tail. **Most important:** never exceed the smoker temperature above 90 F or the salmon will become mushy. Depending on the density of the smoke, the smoking may take anywhere from 6 hrs to two days to complete. The finished fish will have a slight bronze tint.

To test doneness, cut of a small piece from the tail and taste it. The thin, outside piece will taste much smokier that the thicker center.

The finished product may be lightly brushed with oil to inhibit mold growth, and wrapped in paper (plastic would encourage mold). Refrigerated, the fish will keep at least one week. To keep it longer, wrap it snugly in plastic and freeze.

To serve: Using a long, sharp, thin bladed slicing knife start at the tail end. Cut very thin slices at a long angle. Place these in a slightly wrinkled fashion on chilled plates or a platter.

Sprinkle with capers and a thinly sliced red onion, serve with pumpernickel or rye bread.

Smoked salmon is also served as an open face sandwich over cream cheese spread. For elegant appetizers or first course, you may fill slices of salmon with various fillings, such as crabmeat and roll them up into bundles. Or you may simply drape slices over quartered eggs, cream cheese sticks or cucumber wedges. Trimmings and bits of cold salmon make a great dip when pureed in a food processor with cream cheese. Slivers of cold smoked salmon can also be used in salads and various pasta dishes.

SMOKED PEPPERED BLUEFISH

Dry Cure: Use boneless fillets with skin on. Lay them skin side down, sprinkle with sugar and season heavily with Kosher salt and fresh ground black pepper. Place 2 fillets together skin side out and wrap them snugly in plastic.

Set them on a tray, cover with another tray and place a 5 lb weight on top. Refrigerate overnight. Following day un-wrap them, rinse with cold water and place skin side down on racks in a cold room or refrigerator for several hours to dry.

When a shiny surface develops, they are ready for smoking.

To smoke:

Cold smoking process is described in the recipe above.

Failure to maintain low temperature in the smoker will cook the fish.

It will still taste good, but you will not be able to slice it very thin, as it will crumble.

Wrap smoked fish in paper and refrigerate for up to one week. To keep it longer, wrap it in plastic and freeze.

To serve:

Using a sharp, thin, long bladed knife, slice the bluefish, starting at the tail into thin slices. Detach them from the skin, fold each one in half and arrange the slices on plates or a platter. Sprinkle thin sliced red onion rings over and finish with a sprinkling of olive oil and red wine vinegar. Serve as an appetizer, on sandwiches and cold plates.

SMOKED SALMON ROLLS WITH CRABMEAT

If you use crabmeat that has been frozen, squeeze most of its juice out, otherwise the mixture will become watery. Pick the crabmeat over for shell and cartilage fragments; chop up any large chunks. One pound of crabmeat will yield 32 rolls for H.D. or 10-12 larger rolls for first course.

Various sauces may be used, always sparingly, just to bind the crabmeat, so it holds together. Try the Louis or Remoulade or Mustard Sauces (see recipes).

To make rolls, spread very thin slices of salmon on a table. Place a small amount of crabmeat salad at one end and roll up. Dip ends in chopped parsley or dill.

SMOKED FISH DIP

Ends and pieces of cold smoked salmon or bluefish make an excellent dip. They should be pureed for maximum flavor. Hot-smoked fish only needs to be flaked up and deboned.

If you use cold-smoked fish, place all ingredients except chives in a blender or a processor and puree smooth. Last fold in the chives by hand. When using flaked fish, blend dressing ingredients together first, then fold in the fish. For a taste change you may add a little grated onion.

1 cup smoked fish	2 dashes Worcestershire sauce
1/2 cup mayonnaise	2 dashes Tabasco sauce
1 cup sour cream	3 Tbsp finely cut chives

FISH SALAD

Many types of cooked fish as well as crustaceans may be used. Skin, debone and flake the fish first. Cut up lobsters, crab or shrimp.

For 2 cups of flaked fish:

In a bowl mix dressing ingredients together.

Then, stir in the vegetables and last, fold in the fish.

Taste and adjust seasoning.

Uses:

1. Serve as a luncheon, garnished with celery hearts, scallions, radishes, tomato and egg wedges, olives, etc. and hot, crispy rolls.

2. spread on toast points for an appetizer.

3. stuff into tomatoes or heap on avocado halves.

4. use as a sandwich filling.

5. you may also make a hot toast out of it by spreading the salad on a toasted sliced bread, topping it with a little mayonnaise and baking it (about 15 min.) in 400 F oven to piping hot.

Dressing:

1/4 cup mayonnaise

2 Tbsp sour cream

1 Tbsp lemon juice

1 tsp prepared mustard

1/4 cup finely diced celery

1 scallion, finely sliced

salt and pepper

SHELLFISH AND CRUSTACEANS

OYSTER STEW

4 servings

2 cups freshly shucked oysters

4 Tbsp butter

3 cups half and half

pepper to taste

1/4 tsp celery salt

4 drops Worcestershire sauce

paprika

Preheat the serving bowls.

Heat the half and half (milk and cream) to almost a boiling point.

Separately, warm the oysters in butter until their edges curl. Season them and divide between bowls. Add the half and half.

Sprinkle tops with paprika and serve with crackers or warm French bread.

OYSTERS ROCKEFELLER

4 servings

There are many variations of this recipe. Fresh, mild herbs are necessary.

24 oysters

4 Tbsp butter

1/4 cup chopped celery

1/4 cup chopped scallions

1 Tbsp chopped chervil

1/3 cup chopped parsley

1 cup watercress leaves

1 cup spinach leaves

salt, pepper

1/3 cup Pernod (liqueur)

1 stick butter

1/4 cup bread crumbs

Preheat oven to 400 F.

Shuck the oysters leaving them on the deeper shell. Detach them from bottom and place these shells on a bed of rock or other salt on pie plates to keep them level.

Cook celery and scallions in butter until softened, add rest of herbs and spinach, cook to wilt only.

Transfer them to a blender or a processor, with the rest of the butter and seasoning.

Mound this preparation on the oysters, sprinkle with bread crumbs and bake to heat through.

FRIED OYSTERS

4 servings

As with any fried food, the type of fat used for the frying will make a tremendous difference on the flavor of the product. The best is peanut or safflower oil, with some clarified butter (see Walleye Sauté recipe) blended in.

24 large oysters, freshly shucked

flour

3 eggs mixed with 3 Tbsp milk

freshly made cracker crumbs from saltines

salt and pepper to taste

Blend the eggs with the milk.

Drain the oysters, dip them in flour and shake excess off. Then dip them in the egg wash and roll them in the crumbs to coat completely.

Place the oysters on a piece of wax paper.

In a large skillet preheat at least 1/2 inch of fat, place in about a dozen oysters at a time in one layer and not too crowded. Brown them quickly on one side, turn and brown them on the other side. With a wire skimmer or a slotted spoon remove them and place them on paper towel covered tray. Sprinkle them lightly with salt and pepper.

Repeat with the next batch.

Serve with mashed or boiled new potatoes, lemon and a Remoulade sauce (see recipe).

SCALLOPS

We have basically three varieties of native scallops: The sea scallops come from deeper waters off the North Atlantic shore, the sweet, small cape scallops come (in season) from Cape Cod area and the Southern calicos, which are rather mediocre. Scallops are dredged using a steel mesh pouch dragged over the sea floor. They are shucked right on the boat, the shells and entrails dropped back in the water. The so called *diver* scallops are very large sea scallops harvested by divers around rock formations not accessible to dredges. The color of sea scallops ranges from pearly white to light beige, pink and orange and is not indicative of quality or flavor.

Fresh scallops are shiny in appearance, have a pleasant sea smell, firm texture and there is no juice in the container. It is a common practice of unscrupulous producers to soak sea scallops in a solution of salt and chemicals to increase their weight and mask any offensive odor.

Scallops which have been soaked always appear to have "juice" in their containers, look dull white, are flabby and when you buy them, you get *soaked* also!

Scallops when cooked slightly underdone will melt in your mouth. Overcooked scallops will shrink to firm rubbery balls, dry in texture.

BROILED SCALLOPS

Figure about one pound for 2-3 servings.

To broil scallops requires very little preparation.

Preheat a broiler.

Place the scallops in a bowl, season lightly with salt and pepper and add a little melted butter or oil. Mix them, and then place them in one layer on a baking sheet, close together.

Sprinkle them lightly with some bread crumbs and paprika and place 3 inches below the flame. They will be done when they are delicately browned and slightly

undercooked, in about 3 minutes, depending on their size. Overcooked scallops will be rubbery.

Slide a wide spatula under them and without rolling them over, transfer to plates. Serve with lemon, Remoulade sauce (see recipe) and boiled new or mashed potatoes.

SCALLOPS SAUTÉ WITH FRESH HERBS

4 servings

1 1/2 lb scallops

salt and pepper

4 Tbsp clarified butter,

1/2 cup chopped fresh herbs

combined: chives, parsley,

tarragon, chervil

juice of 1/2 lemon

Preheat a large, stick-free skillet or two.

Dry the scallops, and season them.

Add butter to hot pans, then the

scallops in a single layer and over high heat

sear them quickly on all sides, just to heat through.

Add the herbs and lemon juice, toss to coat.

Serve with mashed or boiled potatoes and a salad.

FRIED SCALLOPS

Proceed the same way as in Fried Oysters recipe.

CRABS

Along the Atlantic Coast we have the Blue crabs, which after molting

(shedding their hard shell in order to grow) become Soft shell crabs for a short time.

In the Northern Atlantic we have the Peekytoe and the Jonah crab, which belongs to the Rock crab family. From Florida and Mexico (formerly also Cuba) come the Stone crab claws.

From the Pacific Coast we get the Dungeness crab, from Alaska the King crab and the lesser quality Snow crab. Most crabs come to us already cooked (except the Soft shell), although in some Atlantic regions you may catch your own Blue crab and in Alaska people trap King crabs. To cook a live crab, simmer it in salted water for 8 minutes per pound.

SOFT SHELL CRABS

The season for Soft shell crabs is May and June, although some Blue crabs molt in other months. Frozen Soft shells are available year around. They are priced according to size (measured across the back from point-to-point). The biggest (over 5 1/2 inches) are called whales. The smaller (3 1/2 to 4 inches) are called mediums.

To prepare a live Soft shell crab for cooking: Using scissors snip off the face.

Then lift the two outside points of the shell and remove the gills (spongy matter) underneath.

Last, turn the crab over and pull off its tail, called the apron. Serve two to three crabs per person.

BAKED CRABMEAT TOAST

Use the mushroom stuffing mixture described in

Stuffed Mushroom Caps with Crabmeat."

Toast bread slices on one side (under a grill).

Spread crabmeat mixture about 1/3 inch thick on toasted side, level.

Set slices on a buttered cookie sheet and spread a thin coat of mayonnaise over their top.

Before serving, bake in a 400 F oven for about 10 minutes to brown tops.

For appetizers cut each slice into 6 rectangles.

For a luncheon cut slices diagonally into triangles and serve 3 triangles per serving. Garnish with celery hearts, radishes, tomato wedges, scallions, etc.

CRAB CAKES

Most crab cake recipes call for bread crumbs to bind the mixture together. Crabmeat has a very delicate flavor, which in my opinion is overpowered by the taste of the bread crumbs. For that reason I prefer to use a more natural binder -- pureed scallops or shrimp.

See Fish Stuffing on page 102

In place of scallops you may also use raw shrimp or some firm white-fleshed fish.

Various types of crabmeat can be used. Most common is from Blue crab (called Maryland crabmeat), also King, Peekytoe, King and Dungeness.

Snow crab has poor taste. You may also use cooked chopped shrimp, crayfish, lobster, salmon or other cooked fish.

If you are using crabmeat that has been frozen, squeeze most of its juice out first. Pick it over for shell fragments and tendons. Chop larger chunks up. Mix crabmeat with just enough forcemeat to hold it together. You may add chopped chives, green onions or other herbs, such as tarragon or basil if you wish. Scoop out balls of this mixture on a floured or oiled table and flatten them into cakes.

In a skillet gently brown the cakes in butter or olive oil on both sides.

Serve with a cold or warm sauce, new potatoes and a salad.

LOBSTERS

We have two native species: the so called Maine lobster (*homard* in French), which is the

true lobster and the Florida rock lobster, also called spiny lobster (called *langouste* in other languages), which is claw-less and very good when fresh.

Of the imported, frozen rock lobster tails, there are two basic types:

the cold water ones, which come mostly from Australia and South Africa are top quality.

The warm water lobster tails come to us from Bermuda and are mediocre.

There are several other lobster species around the world. Most are very good when fresh.

BOILED LOBSTER

Live "Maine" lobsters are priced according to size. The one pound and under are called *chicken lobster* and are less expensive than the prime size 1 1/2 to 2 lbs.

One claw lobsters are called culls and are also less expensive and a good buy. Very large lobsters (over 3 lbs) can be tough.

Female lobsters are generally more tender and may contain some eggs. To determine their sex, turn the lobster over and look at the point where the tail is attached to the body. There is a pair of small appendages, which are rigid and longer in the male, soft, hairy and shorter in the female. The female tail is also somewhat wider.

To boil 4 average size lobsters, you need a 1 ½ gallon pot with a lid.

Half fill it with water, add a handful of salt and bring it to a boil.

Drop the lobsters in, upside down, cover the pot and reduce heat to hold it below simmer.

Cook 15 minutes for one pounders. Add 3 minutes more for every 1/2 lb heavier.

When done, remove the lobsters from water. Pull arms with claws off and crack

them using a heavy, flat object. Using a large knife, split bodies into halves, lengthwise.

Remove the stomach (small sack between the eyes) and the intestinal vein in the tail and discard.

Keep the liver (green, soft matter) called tomalley, which experts consider the best part of the lobster. Place on plates and serve with lemon, melted butter and hot French bread.

BROILED LOBSTER

Please see general information about lobsters in Boiled Lobster recipe above.

Preheat a broiler or an oven to 450 F.

Grasp the lobster body with one hand and with the fingers of the other

hand, twist the claws with the attached arms off.

Then place the lobster (flat, tail extended) on a cutting board.

Hold it with your left hand (reverse everything if you are left handed)

with its head pointing to the right. Plunge the point of a large knife straight down into the body and split the front part lengthwise trough the head.

Turn the lobster around and split the rest of it through the tail. You should now have two equal halves. Place them straight side together on a baking sheet.

Remove the stomach (sac between the eyes) and the intestine from the tail and discard. Leave the dark green, soft liver. With a heavy, flat object crack the claws and place them one on each side of the body.

Spoon melted butter over the lobster, season with salt and pepper,

sprinkle lightly with paprika and breadcrumbs.

Broil or bake, basting occasionally with butter about 12-15 minutes

to firm up the meat. Do not overcook, or they become dry and tough.

Serve with lemon and melted butter on the side.

LOBSTER BISQUE

8 servings

2 live lobsters, 2 1/4 to 2 1/2 lb size each   2 qts water

In a large, wide saucepan bring the water to a boil. Drop the lobsters in upside down, cover with lid, reduce the temperature to barely simmer, cook 18 minutes. Lift lobsters out.

When they are cool enough to handle, crack the claws, split bodies lengthwise in halves, remove stomachs (small pouch at the point of head), save the liver (green matter) and any coral if present (red eggs in females) and remove all meat. Set meat, coral and livers aside, covered.

Preheat oven to 400.

Chop up the shells, put them into a roasting pan with 3 Tbsp of butter, place in the oven. Roast the shells, turning them once a while, to a bronze color. When done, put them in a sauce pan and crush them into small pieces. Add 4 cups chicken stock and 2 cups dry white wine.

Bring it to a simmer, cook 20 minutes and strain.

While the stock is cooking, start preparing the soup:

3 Tbsp olive oil	3/4 cup flour
3 Tbsp butter	6 Tbsp cognac
1 Tbsp whole black peppercorns	3/4 cup tomato puree
1 cup chopped onion	the lobster stock

1 cup chopped celery	1 cup heavy cream
3/4 cup chopped carrot	the lobster liver (and coral)
1 Tbsp mashed garlic	salt and pepper
1/2 tsp dried thyme	pinch of cayenne pepper

In a heavy bottom sauce pan, sauté the vegetables and spices in fats until translucent.

Stir in the flour, cook 2 minutes. Add half of the cognac, the puree and stock. Whip to a smooth consistency, bring to a boil, then simmer for 20 minutes. Strain, pressing hard to extract all liquid, place back on stove.

Blend the cream with the lobster liver, then whip it into the soup. Bring it to a simmer, add cognac, taste and adjust seasoning.

Slice the lobster meat into small slices, add to the soup and serve.

SHRIMP

Our native and imported shrimp are sorted by size and color.

The *Gulf shrimp* caught off the coasts of Texas, Florida and Mexico come in sizes from U-10 (under 10) to 60 per pound. The larger they are, the more expensive per pound, but not necessarily better tasting. By color we have the *whites*, which have the least iodine content and are the most expensive, then *pinks, browns,* and *ambers.*

The *tiger* shrimp, once fished off the California Coast now come mostly from the Far East, are farm raised in fresh water ponds and their taste and texture are not as good as the Gulf shrimp.

Very large shrimp are sometimes called prawns, although that term properly belongs to a species found in the Irish Sea. The small Alaskan and Icelandic shrimp will go to 120 per pound and are fairly bland tasting.

Spanish *red shrimp* have a spectacular color, are very expensive, but their bland taste and soft texture leave a lot to be desired.

We also have *Rock shrimp*, from Florida and Mexico, which resemble miniature lobster tails, available fresh in season. Their frozen shelled meat is available year around.

COOKING SHRIMP FOR COLD DISHES

As with all fish, shrimp should not be really boiled, but only poached (cooked at a temperature below simmering). Boiling will make them crumbly. Regardless of what some cookbooks or package directions say, always thaw shrimps before cooking, either in a refrigerator or under cold, running water. Dropping a 5 lb block of frozen shrimp into boiling water will cool the water down, then overcook shrimp on the outside of the package, before the inside will thaw out.

For 5 lbs. of shrimp make the following:

Court Bouillon:

1 gallon water	Bring it all to a boil, cook 10 minutes, then stir in
1/2 cup salt	the shrimp. Cover, reduce heat to low and hold
1/4 cup sugar	about 3 minutes. Then remove one large shrimp
2 bay leaves	and break it in half to look inside. If there is no
1/2 small onion, sliced	translucency drain the shrimps, chill them briefly
1 Tbsp celery seed	with cold water and drain again.
1 Tbsp cracked	Peel and devein them while still warm.
black pepper	

To keep them well, place cooked shrimp in a sealed container and refrigerate in the coldest part of the refrigerator. Never keep cooked shrimp in water, or directly on ice, as they will bloat and turn mushy. Before using, sprinkle them with a little lemon juice and rinse them with cold water.

Shrimp cocktail: Serve with a sauce of your choice. (See sauces in back of book)

SHRIMP AND AVOCADO BOATS

Serve as a light luncheon or as a first course at dinner. Select ripe, but not mushy avocados. Peel them and cut in halves. Remove pits, cut a sliver off the round side to make them sit flat without tipping over. Spoon a little sauce (see recipes) into the pit hollow. Arrange cooked shrimps (see recipe) over top, spoon more sauce over. For luncheon, garnish with egg and tomato wedges, olives.

Recommended sauces to serve: Louis or cocktail (see recipes).

STIR-FIRED SHRIMP

with Chinese black bean sauce

6 servings

Note: in place of shrimp, you may also use lobster, scallops, sturgeon, Dover sole or other

firm fleshed fish.

2 1/2 lb shrimp   Peel and devein the shrimp, save shells; refrigerate shrimp.

Sauce:

3 Tbsp canola oil	Preheat oven to 400 F.
1/4 cup carrots, sliced	Preheat a wide, 2 qt saucepan, add oil
1/4 cup onion, sliced	stir in the shrimp shells
1/4 cup leek, white part, sliced	place in oven for 15-20 minutes until
1/4 cup celery, sliced	shells turn to bronze tint. Remove from oven,
1/2 Tbsp red pepper flakes	stir in vegetables and seasonings, sauté to
1 bay leaf	translucent, then add clam juice, broth and wine.
1 tsp thyme	Bring to a boil, simmer 20 min. and strain.
1 tsp black peppercorns	Reduce by boiling to 1 cup.
1 cup clam juice	Add the black bean sauce and starch with
1 cup chicken broth	sherry, bring back to a boil, remove from
1/4 cup dry white wine	stove, set aside.

1/2 cup black bean sauce with garlic (Chinese condiment)

2 Tbsp corn starch mixed with

3 Tbsp sherry wine

Final preparation:

Please read instructions on stir-frying in *Cooking Definitions*

2 Tbsp peanut oil	Preheat a stick-free wok or skillet to hot. Swirl in the oil and
salt to taste, if needed	only enough shrimp to cover the bottom in one layer.
vegetables: 6 cups in total,	Brown lightly on one side, turn over and

all in bite-size pieces: asparagus,

pea pods, scallions, water chestnuts

and mushrooms.

brown lightly on the other side. After all the shrimp are

done, lift them out and set them aside. Add the stir-fry

vegetables to the same pan, cook briefly to *al dente*.
Then add the sauce, reheat and fold the shrimp back in.
Taste and adjust seasoning.

Serve over steamed rice (see recipe) or plain noodles.

SCAMPI

4 servings

2 lbs peeled and deveined shrimp
3 Tbsp olive oil

1 tsp paprika
salt & pepper

1/4 cup dry sherry wine

In a skillet heat the oil, add shrimp, garlic, paprika and seasoning.

Sauté shrimp until they turn color.
Add wine, cook to done and juice

is emulsified (looks thickened).
Serve over steamed rice.

CURRIED SHRIMP

4 servings

The flavor of this dish will largely depend on the type and quality of the curry powder.

Most domestic curries leave a bitter aftertaste. Some imported ones are really hot!

I have had best success with *Sun Brand Madras Curry Powder*, imported from India.

2 lbs shrimp, peeled and deveined

3 Tbsp butter

3 med. onions, finely chopped

4 Tbsp curry powder

salt to taste

2 medium bananas, mashed

Sauté the shrimps in butter to almost done.

Remove them with a slotted spoon and keep

warm. Add the onions to the remaining

butter in the pan and sauté to translucent.

Add the curry and stir over heat 20 seconds,

add bananas, cream of coconut and chicken

4 Tbsp coconut milk

1/2 cup chicken stock

1 cup yogurt

stock, simmer 15 minutes.

Whip in yogurt, add shrimp and reheat,

but do not boil.

Taste and adjust seasoning.

Serve over steamed rice (see recipe) with Major Gray (mango) chutney on the side.

ROCK SHRIMP

From the Gulf Coast of Florida and Mexico come rock shrimp,

which due to their hard shell look like miniature lobster tails.

Their taste also reminds us of a lobster, more so than shrimp.

They are available fresh in season, either with their shells on

or peeled and deveined, which make great sauté dishes, pasta items and cold salads.

Frozen rock shrimp meat is available year round and can be used anywhere in place of

peeled and deveined "regular" shrimp.

I like them best as:

BROILED ROCK SHRIMP IN SHELL, WITH GARLIC BUTTER

3 Tbsp mashed garlic + 1/2 cup melted butter or olive oil

Preheat a broiler. You will need at least 1/2 lb of rock shrimp per serving.

With a knife split the upper shell, cutting through the meat down to,

but not through the bottom shell. Pull the two halves open, place shrimp on a baking sheet and

season with salt and pepper.

Prepare enough garlic butter or oil to coat them generously.

Spoon it over them, then sprinkle lightly with paprika.

Broil them to delicately brown and meat firmed up.

Serve with hot French bread or rolls and a salad.

CRAYFISH

Crayfish, sometimes called crawfish or crawdads is a freshwater relative of a lobster. For cooking purposes we recognize two species: the Eastern type so popular in Louisiana and the much bigger and meatier Western crayfish, native to California, Oregon and Washington State. They can be served alone, with melted butter and also make great soups, sauces and various dishes.

We boil them first:

Bring some salted water to a boil.

Grasp a live crayfish with your left hand (reverse procedure for left-handed persons) with the tail pointing to the right. With your right hand, grasp the center "wing" blade of the tail end. Twist it to one side, then the other and then pull out the intestine. Drop the crayfish into the boiling water. Lower the heat and simmer 5-8 minutes. Drain.

To eat: crack the shells, remove meat.

Serve with Remoulade or tartar sauce (see recipes).

CLAMS

On the Atlantic Coast, the only hard shell clams sold for consumption are all from the *quahog* specie. The *quahog* harvesting methods have changed little since pre- Colonial days as clam fishermen work from skiffs, using long handled rakes (bull rakes) digging for clams on the ocean bottom. They are sold and priced according to four size categories. The smallest, most tender and the most expensive are the *littlenecks*, then *top necks*, *cherrystones* and the largest are the chewier *quahogs*, which are chopped for use in chowders, stuffed clams and clam cakes.

The smaller size clams are also served raw, on the half shell same as oysters.

Then there are the soft-shell *steamer clams*, favored in New England clam bakes.

On the Pacific Coast, there are several edible varieties, notably the *razor clam, mud clam* and the giant *geoduck* (called gooey-duck), which are not sold commercially.

CLAMS CASINO

4 servings

6 strips of bacon

24 littleneck clams

1/3 cup softened butter

1/4 cup chopped shallots

1/4 cup chopped parsley

2 Tbsp finely chopped green pepper

2 Tbsp finely chopped red pepper

1 tsp lemon juice

dash of Worcestershire sauce

Preheat oven to 450 F.

Cook bacon only until edges start to brown, leaving it still soft. Cut each slice into 4 pieces. Set aside.

Mix butter with the rest of ingredients together,

spoon over clams.

Top with bacon pieces and bake to crisp the bacon and heat clams through.

STEAMED CLAMS

For a meal, figure about two dozen soft shell clams per person. Scrub them well before cooking. Place about a half inch of salted water on the bottom of the pot, bring to a boil, place the clams in and cover tightly. Steam about 6-8 minutes, tossing over, until they open.

Discard any unopened clams. Serve them in bowls, their broth and melted butter in separate cups on the side. Serve with crusty French bread or rolls.

To eat, pick up each clam by the neck (foot), pull it out of the shell, dip in butter or juice and holding it with your teeth pull the dark covering off the neck and discard.

MUSSELS

Most mussels sold nowadays are the native *blue mussel* variety cultivated on ropes suspended from floating platforms, which minimize sand entering into them. There are also the much larger *green mussels* available, imported from New Zealand. When buying mussels, select tightly closed ones, with pleasant ocean smell. Keep them refrigerated, covered with sea weed, a wet towel or wet newspapers until needed. Before cooking, soak them in cold, salted water for an hour, then rinse them with clean water. Discard any open ones. With the help of a paring knife, rip the beards (fibers) off and discard. Most mussels are eaten steamed, however excellent soups and sauces can be made with mussels.

STEAMED MUSSELS WITH GARLIC AND HERBS

6 servings

2 qts mussels

1 cup dry white wine

3 Tbsp chopped shallots

2 Tbsp chopped garlic

1 Tbsp cracked black pepper

1 tsp leaf thyme

In a stainless saucepan with a tight fitting lid
Bring wine, shallots, garlic, pepper and thyme
to a boil. Add mussels and cover tightly.
When steam begins to escape, using a towel
grasp pan with lid and toss mussels inside to turn them
over. Steam another minute and check them.

1 stick unsalted butter

3 Tbsp chopped fresh herbs-
chives, tarragon, parsley

As soon as the mussels open, lift them out to
another dish and keep them warm, covered.
Strain juice through a fine sieve or cloth to a
smaller pan, keeping any sand on the bottom back.

Reduce juice by boiling to 1/2 cup. Using a wire whisk, whip butter piece by piece into the juice. Last add the chopped fresh herbs. Check mussels for any remaining beards and pull one shell off each.

Place mussels on half shells in deep plates, spoon butter-juice over and serve with hot French bread and a nice dry white wine.

MUSSELS AND CORN CHOWDER

6 servings

18 mussels

3 ears of corn

1/3 cup thinly sliced leek, white part only

1/3 cup small diced carrot

1/3 cup small diced onion

3 Tbsp butter

½ cup flour

4 cups chicken broth

1 cup mussel broth

salt and pepper to taste

corn

¾ cup heavy cream

2 Tbsp finely cut chives

Cook the mussels the same way as in the recipe above.

Cut the kernels off the corn cobs, set aside.

In a heavy sauce pan, melt butter,

add vegetables, sauté to translucent.

Add flour, stir for 2 minutes, whip

in chicken broth and mussel broth,

bring to a simmer, cook 15 minutes.

Season with salt a pepper.

Add corn kernels, bring to a boil.

Add cream and mussels, sprinkle

with chives and serve.

SNAILS (ESCARGOTS)

In Central Europe, there is a fair abundance of various snails and slugs (some are huge), possibly due to wetter and milder climate. In late fall, to survive winter without food, the snails draw themselves into their shells, then seal the opening with a hardened crust. In that stage, the edible snails are sold in markets. In the winter, we may find fresh, live snails in some of our Italian stores.

The canned escargot could be a land snail, mostly imported from Europe, or a swamp snail that comes from the Far East (disdained by the French). There is some limited production of small land snails (*petit gris* variety) in California also. Most snails though come to us already cooked, in cans, usually with the shells included in a separate bag.

The *helix* species of French import is the most expensive, but is not an assurance of best taste. Just because they were *packed* in France does not guarantee that they were actually grown in France. Some Far Eastern snails I have tasted were better than the helix snails at half the price. The extra-large are more expensive than smaller size.

The simplest way to prepare cooked snails is as follows:

Preheat oven to 450 F.

1 cup softened butter	Cream first 5 ingredients together. Put a little butter
6 cloves garlic, chopped	in each shell, push the snail in and close with
½ cup chopped parsley	more butter. Place them with the shell opening up
¼ cup chopped walnuts	on baking dishes, sprinkle with crumbs.
1 Tbsp dry white wine	Bake them to bubbly hot.
2 Tbsp bread crumbs	Serve with hot rolls and white wine.

You may also serve them without shells, just heated through in the butter.

There are also edible sea snails. The tiny, tender ones from cold waters are called periwinkles and are used as appetizers, in sauces and as a garnish. The large one from tropical waters is the chewy conch, used mostly in chowders.

SECTION- MUSHROOMS

MUSHROOMS

When purchasing fresh mushrooms, select firm, pleasantly smelling, dry to the touch mushrooms. The domestic button variety comes in white or brown. They taste the same. When old, mushrooms turn dark, sticky and ammonia smelling and they can become poisonous.

Avoid canned mushrooms of any kind, as they have no flavor or aroma.

Edible wild mushrooms, with the exception of truffles, should always be cooked. Some species, such as false morels and honey-caps contain small amount of toxins, which dissipate during cooking. Keep fresh mushrooms in an open paper bag or a basket, to allow them to breathe, refrigerated. Keeping them wrapped in plastic will speed up spoiling.

Wash mushrooms just before cooking, agitating them gently in a large amount of water. Then lift them out and drain. Never soak the mushrooms for more than a minute, as they will absorb a lot of water. Then check them over for any soil still clinging to the stems. Wiping button mushrooms with a damp towel only makes sense if you are going to serve them raw, whole, as they will keep white longer. Hollow mushrooms, such as morels should be split in halves to check the inside for insects, slugs and other creatures hiding there. (I have found a baby salamander in a morel).

Different wild mushrooms contain various amounts of water. Shiitakes are very dry and therefore suitable for grilling. Morels on the other hand are very wet, so they are better suited for other forms of cooking. We have to take these attributes into cooking consideration.

TO PRESERVE MUSHROOMS,

we may either dry them or freeze them. Thin bodied mushrooms such as morels may be strung up on strings in a warm, breezy place to dry. Meatier mushrooms, such as bolets (also called porcini, cepes, steinpilze) have to be thinly sliced and spread on paper to dry, turning them over once. When completely dry, store them in cloth satchels. Keeping them in closed containers will cause them to mildew, unless they are kept in a freezer. Dried mushrooms have a different, more pungent taste and are best suited for flavoring soups and sauces, but because of their leathery consistency, they are not suitable for side dishes.

Firm mushrooms, such as shiitakes, bolets and truffles may be frozen raw. Some people freeze whole breaded morels. To cook them they drop them frozen into a deep fryer so they firm up, before thawing. Frozen bolets are best sliced semi-frozen and cooked before they thaw. Most raw frozen mushrooms though will turn into a mush when thawed out. For that reason, to preserve mushrooms for future use, it is best to sauté sliced fresh mushrooms in butter or olive oil first, allowing most juice to evaporate. When cold, they are packed in plastic bags and closed tightly, eliminating all air in the bags and frozen. When thawed, they will taste close to fresh mushrooms and their consistency suitable for most preparations.

MUSHROOMS SAUTÉ WITH MADEIRA AND GARLIC

6 appetizer servings

2 lbs button mushrooms	Cut large mushrooms in halves or quarters.
4 Tbsp butter or olive oil	Heat butter or oil in a skillet, add garlic and mushrooms,
1 Tbsp chopped garlic	sauté for 30 seconds, add wine and seasonings.
4 Tbsp Madeira wine	Bring to a boil, cover and allow to steam 1-2 minutes.
salt and pepper to taste	Then remove the lid and cook to reduce the juice to a glaze.
1 Tbsp chopped parsley	Remove from fire, sprinkle with parsley and serve as a side
	dish, first course, on toast or on steaks or veal cutlets.

Note: You may sauté any type of edible mushrooms in this manner.

For variety, omit wine, add a touch of cognac and cream.

ABOUT FISH SAUCES AND GARNISHES

Selecting the right sauce and garnish to be served with the fish will make the meal far more enjoyable.

Cold or warm sauces may be served with warm fish, but only cold sauces with cold fish. As a rule, lean fish tend to be milder tasting and we serve them with milder sauces, if any. A poached, white fleshed fish will be complemented with some type of creamy, white wine based sauce, perhaps finished with fresh herbs, such as dill, chives or tarragon.

Oilier, strong tasting fish benefit from bold tasting, acidy and spicy sauces, salsas and garnishes.

For the starch, you cannot go wrong serving boiled potatoes with any warm fish.

While they may sound mundane, you can make them taste and look very good.

To make ordinary boiled potatoes fancy, shape them into large olives or mushrooms.

Simple small new, fingerling or red skin potatoes, cooked in the skin taste great.

When boiling potatoes, add only enough water to not quite cover them.

Less water will intensify their flavor. Add salt and a little caraway seed when cooking them.

Do not hold boiled potatoes in water to keep them warm. Cook them when you need them.

Spoon melted butter with chopped parsley, dill or chives over cooked potatoes.

With very few exceptions, casserole type potatoes and vegetables do not go very well with fish, as their flavors clash.

COLD SAUCES AND DRESSINGS

BASIC STANDARD DRESSING

We use this dressing in many fish, meat, poultry, pasta and vegetable salads. It is also used as a base for many cold sauces. Stir together:

1 cup mayonnaise

2 Tbsp Dijon mustard

pinch of cayenne pepper

6 Tbsp sour cream

2 Tbsp lemon juice

dash of Worcestershire sauce

Could be made well in advance. Will keep refrigerated for up to three weeks.

For fresh herb sauces, such as dill, tarragon, chive, basil, parsley, chervil, etc.,

add enough finely chopped fresh herbs to Standard Dressing to achieve the desired flavor.

To intensify green color, machine blend the sauce with one or two spinach leaves.

To thin these sauces, use white wine or coffee cream.

TARTAR SAUCE

To 1 ½ cups of Standard Dressing, add:

1 hardboiled egg, chopped

2 Tbsp chopped scallions

2 Tbsp chopped sour pickles

2 Tbsp chopped parsley

REMOULADE SAUCE

To 1 1/2 cups Standard Dressing add:

finely grated zest of 1/2 lemon

2 Tbsp chopped capers

4 Tbsp chopped sour gherkins

2 tsp chopped fresh tarragon

2 Tbsp finely chopped onion

2 Tbsp chopped parsley

1 anchovy fillet, mashed

LOUIS SAUCE

To 1 cup Standard Dressing add: 1/3 cup ketchup 2 Tbsp cognac or brandy

This sauce enhances crab, lobster, shrimp, salmon, crayfish and other cold fish.

COCKTAIL SAUCE

Stir together:

1/2 cup chili sauce

1/2 cup ketchup

1 Tbsp Dijon mustard

1/2 tsp Worcestershire sauce

3 Tbsp prepared horseradish

1/4 tsp ground black pepper

Used mostly for oysters, shrimp cocktail, also crab.

MUSTARD SAUCE

1 tsp dry mustard

1 Tbsp lemon juice

1 Tbsp white wine

1/4 cup Dijon mustard

1 cup mayonnaise

In a bowl stir dry mustard with lemon juice to a smooth paste. Add the rest.

Serve with crab, shrimp and other seafood. Keep refrigerated.

APPLE HORSERADISH

1/2 cup prepared horseradish (store bought)

1 to 1 1/2 cups peeled and finely grated apples (Granny Smith works best)

pinch of sugar if desired

Place the horseradish in a non-corrosive bowl, grate the apple in and mix immediately to prevent browning. Serve with smoked fish, also pork and duck roasts, boiled beef and ham.

Can be made ahead. W ill keeps for at least a week refrigerated.